On to Alaska

The Pioneer Period in Anchorage Church History

by

M. R. Korody

Beacon Hill Press of Kansas City
Kansas City, Missouri

10   9   8   7   6   5   4   3   2   1

DEDICATED TO

Martha Lorene Korody, a true pioneer, faithful and loving wife who always gives her all for her Lord and His church. Without her inspiration these words would not have been written.

Contents

Contents

Preface

This is our response to many requests from those whose lives touched ours in Anchorage, Alaska, from 1949 to 1963.

To compile a book from pictures, newsprint, magazines, scrapbooks, and church bulletins from every week of those years required a lot of time. Ten years ago, when the publishers asked me to write it, pastoring was a full-time commitment, and I could not do it. It has taken three years in retirement.

My heartfelt thanks to Burdie Strait McLain, whose untiring work typing, correcting, editing, and encouraging has made this task easier to complete. My longhand (in which the first draft was written) is not easy to read when cold, even by myself.

Best of all, Burdie was one of the young mothers and housewives of our Anchorage ministry. Her beautiful witness for Christ then and love for God and people now always shines through. What a lift to us when she volunteered for this task.

My family and I hope you enjoy this chronicle as much as we enjoyed reliving the events of those pioneering years.

—M. R. K.

PUBLISHER'S NOTE: For the 1988-89 missionary reading program, this book has been abridged from a handwritten manuscript of over 350 pages. The manuscript, which will eventually become a part of our church archives, contains a more detailed chronological and historical documentation of the work in establishing the Church of the Nazarene in Anchorage, Alaska. Such church planting was, at that time, under the jurisdiction of the Department of Foreign Missions, and Alaska was still a territory.

In the abridging process, many names and events have had to be omitted from this book, but their contributions and assistance are not overlooked or minimized in this Alaskan outreach.

During the time span of this book, Alaska became a state, and a fifth child, Ileana Marie, became a part of the Korody family.

1

Roots in the Red and White Sand

Our little Sayre, Okla., church, with its open-jet gas flame for winter heat and every window pushed to its maximum opening for summer air that did not always cooperate, is still a refreshing memory of the red and white sands of Oklahoma on the North Fork of the Little Canadian River. It was 1948, and my second pastorate was booming with activity. Our four children, ages two to seven, made their contribution to our busy lives.

Our church had grown to capacity, and we were happy young pastors having the time of our lives with people who were willing to put up with many mistakes and "green" ministry because we were having a beautiful love relationship with a people with whom we wanted to spend the rest of our lives.

Newly ordained and less than four years out of rigid training in the Roman Catholic and Greek Catholic churches by wonderful immigrant parents, I was still learning every day, with my beautiful blue-eyed young wife (now the mother of four wriggling, eager-for-life children), about people, church boards, responsibilities to a community, and my place in all this as a father and pastor.

My former plans to pursue a career in hotel work or disc jockeying were changed when the Lord saved my wife and me at the old Quindaro Church in Kansas City, Kans. A Nazarene had invited us to attend a revival while I was working in the northside machine shop of Sheffield Steel. The speaker delivered the first gospel message I'd ever heard, despite my deeply religious background. Lorene and I gave our hearts to God, the Lord called me into the ministry, and we were pastoring within a year.

My ministry was going so well at the church in Sayre I would have been content to stay there the rest of my life. God had a different idea. He set His plan in motion one day while I was in my little office reading the latest issue of the *Herald of Holiness*. One particular blurb caught my attention: "We have just stopped for refueling in Anchorage, Alaska, from Japan. It would be wonderful if God would put it on the heart of some young pastor to come to this seaport town of 4,000." It was signed by John Stockton and Dr. Orville Nease.

I had Collier's Atlas on my desk and opened it to North America. Alaska seemed a long way from Oklahoma. I located Anchorage and made a pencil mark. Nestled between Cook Inlet and the Chugach mountain range, it was one of the few places listed on the Alaska map.

My boyhood memories of reading books by Zane Grey and stories of the North by James Oliver Curwood sparked my imagination. "Why not?" I said, and dropped to my knees by the office chair to pray about the needs in Anchorage and a person to pioneer this coastal area.

The praying came easily, and I felt good about my part in this. It seemed to be a casual request from two of God's servants at a remote rest stop on their way home from Japan.

The next morning I spent my usual time in personal meditation and sermon preparation. I picked the Collier Atlas up to put it back in my library and on impulse opened it to North America. There were my pencil marks, one on Anchorage and another on Oklahoma. I felt drawn to pray again.

"How easy it is to pray about this," I said to myself. "God must have someone in mind." I rejoiced in the Holy Spirit's witness to my heart that I was on to something.

The following morning I included the matter again in my personal prayer and devotion time. As I thought about Alaska my pulse quickened and emotion gripped me. I felt obligated to pray for someone to obey God and go to Anchorage.

After going through this for several days and enjoying the freedom that accompanied the experience, the emphasis changed. One morning when I opened the atlas to Alaska, an overwhelming conviction seized me about God's man for Anchorage. *I knew it was me.*

No one seemed to know much about Alaska except that the Nazarenes had mission work in Nome, situated on the Bering Sea near Russia, and Fairbanks in the Arctic Circle, around 450 miles north of Anchorage.

I decided to write Nazarene headquarters, explain my call, and find out more. In less than a week, I received a letter from Dr. Hardy C. Powers. He asked me for more personal background and assured me there was a real interest at head-quarters in opening the coast of Alaska.

All this time I was trying not to appear too excited, but I was beginning to perplex my wife who had put down deep roots in the red sand of Oklahoma. She could see a restless-ness in me that even I could not.

One sticky late August day in 1948, I received another let-ter indicating that if funds were available there were possibil-ities ahead in the matter.

Armed with this letter, I crossed the 40 feet separating my church office and the parsonage back door. Lorene was in the kitchen, rolling out biscuits for supper. It was Oklahoma hot. When I saw her, my heart sank. Even in this weather I knew she was content in her little home with her children and a congregation that loved her.

In my brightest tone of voice I said, "Butch (a nickname only I could use), how would you like to go to Alaska?"

She never looked up, but wiped her hands as she went to our wall phone. Holding down the switch hook she said, "Is this the Sayre Ice Company? Would you please send me a 300-pound cake of ice? Just put it in the living room. My husband needs to sit on it."

I shook the letter a little and urged her to read. After a few moments, the tears began to flow, "Honey," she said, "I'll go with you anywhere. Just be sure God's Holy Spirit is directing you."

The work in Alaska was still under the leadership of the Nazarene Foreign Missionary Society. All appointees were personally interviewed by the Board of General Superintendents and voted upon. Funds came from General Budget allocations for foreign missions.

In February I received this letter from Dr. Powers:

Dear Brother Korody,

Your letter was received. I was so glad to hear from you again. I just received some information today that makes it possible for us to go ahead with our plans. So you may take this as your official appointment to the pastorate (to open this work) at Anchorage.

The salary, as I told you, will be $50.00 per week, plus $25.00 a month fuel allowance.

The church will pay your moving expenses to Anchorage and also return after your service there, if you so desire.

However, we are thinking in terms of four or five years if you accept the appointment. I think this should be the basis of our planning. The living quarters, which we own, are furnished of course.

The appointment is subject to a thorough physical examination of each member of your family, and the endorsement of your doctor for this move. That is, we want his opinion as to whether this move would jeopardize the life or the health of any member of your family.

These examinations should be separate and thorough and should be taken some time in March or April if you do not resign [the present pastorate] until a later date.

In other words, we should have this medical examination and your doctor's OK in hand before you tell your people or resign from your work there.

Of course, the first step will be to contact your district superintendent and get his permission to resign your church.

Give him plenty of time to fill your place there.

Before this is done, make sure you have your medical examinations and my acceptance of them before you make a move there locally.

Now, Brother Korody, as I told you before, we simply cannot afford to make a mistake again. We cannot afford to fail in Anchorage, and if I thought there was any hesitation on the part of you or your wife about undertaking this job and carrying through until we establish a work there, then certainly I would not make this appointment because our experience in the past in sending men to Anchorage has not been a happy one.

However, I feel perfectly confident you are God's man for this task, and He will help you and see you through. I believe if you did not feel this way, you would tell me frankly before we become involved in it.

May the Lord bless you and your fine little

family. Let me know how the examinations come out.

The salary of $50.00 a week plus $25.00 for fuel was only a little more than I was receiving in Oklahoma, and we were barely getting by. But I reassured my wife, "God has called us and will make a way."

We passed our physicals easily, even though our family doctor kept muttering something about how a denomination should be exposed that sent young children (ages two to seven) into such a forbidding country.

After sending the results of our physical examinations to Kansas City, we drove to headquarters to be interviewed by the Board of General Superintendents. I faced four of them who tried to set me at ease and yet probed deeply to find any overlooked detail.

My wife and I were interrogated separately. When I was through, she climbed the spiral stairway for her interview. They must have been charmed by her because in one-third of the time she returned all smiles and said Dr. Powers wished to see me. He was ready to give his final approval.

Telling my district superintendent was difficult. He had trouble accepting my sanity. I assured him that the same Lord who had called me to Oklahoma was now calling me to Alaska. He was a good man, a good district superintendent, and his only concern was our welfare. Besides, who had ever heard of Anchorage, or even Alaska?

Telling our beloved congregation about our appointment was even worse. It was one of the hardest things I have had to do. Undoubtedly, they were some of the most wonderful people one could pastor. Because they believed in us, they rallied around in tearful support.

The next step was to tell our parents. My parents had had little contact with me since I left my Greek Catholic home. My conversion had angered them. I had antagonized them further by praying with my father on his deathbed and interfering, they thought, with the parish priest's duties. I knew they would be opposed.

My wife's parents had also shown their contempt for our conversion. They did not want their daughter to marry a Catholic, even though they had no religious training to offer her. Catholicism, though, was better than getting involved with a bunch of "holy rollers." Now I was taking their four grandchildren to Alaska, and they were furious.

Word came from headquarters that I should fly to Anchorage alone to check things out. From early May until mid-June it is not comfortable if you have to be outside very long. Spring breakup is a joyous time in Alaska, but not without raw, cold rain and occasional snow – bad weather for small children.

My wife settled the question even after she knew I meant to drive up there over the unfinished Alaska Highway. She smilingly said, "I'm going, too. We are all going together."

I knew she had God's confirmation about her place at my side. There would be no point in discussing the matter further. I did not even bother to explain this to headquarters.

2

Whoever Heard of the Alcan?

We had had little contact with anyone in Anchorage, but on April 4, 1949, we received the following letter from Sergeant Carlton and his wife, Nazarenes who were stationed at Fort Richardson on the outskirts of the city:

Dear Friends,

The house is not livable and will have to be torn down completely. Above all, *do not* bring the family up here until things are lined up.

Sorry if I may have led you to believe by anything I have said that the picture was not as bad as it was presented for you. Anchorage is tough but needs a Nazarene church badly.

Another acquaintance, who had some background as a Nazarene, surfaced only long enough to contact us when he learned of our plans. He sent the following telegram: "Don't come. It's no place for a family to live, and besides, the place you are supposed to stay in should be torn down or have a match set to it."

But I had made up my mind to go. I was sure God would make a way since He was directing. And so our plans continued.

Everything had to be crated for overseas shipment – first by rail to Seattle, then by boat to Seward, and again by rail to Anchorage.

We left nothing behind and were so glad later. When packing was nearly complete and we'd forgotten our new broom, one of the men pried a board loose and pushed it into a large crate. Sweeping debris out of the shack in Anchorage, I thanked God for that broom.

I received word from Dr. Powers that a schedule was slated for several churches in Oklahoma and Texas to raise $2,500 to help us purchase a new station wagon. Four services raised $750 in cash and pledges. When the balance did not come in, I bought a 1949 Plymouth station wagon and signed a contract for $75.00 monthly payments.

There had been some concern across the church over what seemed to be "a Nazarene Folly." The high prices for heating oil, building materials, and labor in Fairbanks and Nome had drained finances for missions in the frozen North. Dr. Chapman was not enthusiastic about more money for this venture. It had failed twice on the coast. One man stayed three days and another man stayed three months.

We said our good-byes in Oklahoma, and it was hard to leave. To make matters worse, all four children contracted measles and delayed us several days. Finally we piled them into the back of the station wagon, which we had made into a bed of sorts, and headed north.

What a time of emotion! It was an easy time to second-guess my decision – four sick kids, a weary wife with that "Are you sure, honey?" look, my district superintendent telling me it was not too late to back out, and friends, parents, and parishioners left behind weeping.

No one seemed to know anything about the area where we were going or how we were going to get there. The ones writing from up North seemed to be saying one thing: "Stay home!" But my times alone with God only reinforced my conviction in this call. I promised Him I would obey.

We stopped in Kansas City and met with Dr. Powers for a briefing about our trip. Originally we had been ticketed on the ocean-going steamer, the *Baranof*, which was making its last voyage from Seattle to Anchorage. At the last minute we decided to drive instead. That change of plans, to go across Canada on the still-uncompleted Alaska Highway, came close to costing our lives.

While in Kansas City we had a brief and tearful visit with my wife's parents. My father-in-law built us a dust-proof cover of sheet metal for our small trailer loaded with luggage. It was hinged and could be locked, which was important for the 5,000-mile journey.

From Kansas City we drove to Kankakee, Ill., where I preached to newly acquired Olivet Nazarene College and picked up an eight-man squad tent. The tent, which was Dr. Powers' suggestion, proved to be our first home when we arrived in Anchorage.

An African missionary gave us a full-length bearskin coat, saying, "I believe God wants you to have this. It was given to me, but Africa is no place for a bearskin coat." I was to bless God and thank Him for Brother Miller and that stop in Kankakee many times on that perilous and cold highway trip.

We skirted across the corner of Wisconsin, where we bought some cheese. When I seemed to be the only one who cared for it, I stored the cheese in the glove compartment. It was forgotten for several days as we crossed Minnesota and the Devils Lake area of North Dakota. It was rediscovered in Montana's hot rangeland when everyone wondered why an awful odor seemed to be following us. My wife solved the mystery as she opened the glove compartment and heaved the now-whiskered and potent cheese out on the Montana prairie. Even the coyotes would steer clear of it, she declared.

When we arrived at the Canadian border, the officials appeared skeptical as they viewed our family of six. Checking our gear and equipment, they warned us of the unfinished highway. They asked to see our traveler's checks to make sure we had enough money to get back home if we had a breakdown.

The officials did assure us the roads were good to Edmonton, Red Deer, and Dawson Creek. These were our first scheduled stops, and our first contact with Canadians.

We drove to Red Deer College Church without incident and found the people delightful. The pastor was also the college president, and we were able to meet and speak to the small but interested group of students who kept asking why we were going to the forbidden Northland and driving on an unfinished highway. I didn't have profound answers, but they accepted my simple explanation that God was sending us.

The long spring days of mid-May helped us, even if most lakes and streams were still frozen. We arrived in Edmonton just in time to secure a motel but with no time to eat before the Wednesday-night service. The pastor was gone and the laymen didn't know about our coming. They told me to preach anyway, and as I explained our call I noticed some whispering and shaking of heads.

I almost apologized for being there until I received the $7.00 that came in the offering. It went toward a fried-chicken dinner later than evening. My wife lamented it might be the last chicken dinner we would have for a while. She was right.

After Edmonton we drove on gravel road for most of the way to Dawson Creek, where a delightful newlywed couple was pastoring. This young couple, the Arnold Airharts, would become prominent pastors, and he later would be president of Canadian Nazarene College.

They told us horror stories about people who were forced to turn back after traveling a few hundred miles into Alaska. They pleaded with us not to go on. At least stay until the weather warms up and the ground dries, they said. I was wishing we could wait but knew we should arrive and get our roots

18

down before winter set in again. So with extra gas strapped to an already barnacled station wagon, we started up the famous Alcan Highway.

The tales that came back down the highway from Canadian and U.S. road crews, mingled with stories of civilian adventures, would fill a good-sized book. One family of four had lost the trail that was the road, only to be crushed in their Volkswagen by an earthmover that had topped a ridge and didn't see them until too late. Heavy machinery was everywhere.

There was talk of "frost boils," which were hot thermals where tons of rock for the roadbed were dumped and disappeared. Some speculated that drivers who had registered at the Canadian border coming in, and never registered at the Alaska border going out, had fallen into one of these.

The most frightening tale was true without a doubt. Services for food, lodging, and fuel in 1948-49 were 200 or more miles apart.

At least as we left the last paved road on the outskirts of Dawson Creek, we were not on a tight schedule for the remainder of the journey. We had planned to visit only two missionaries along the way. The first was in a town called High Prairie, the second in Fairbanks.

I learned quickly that the one-wheeled luggage trailer would be dragging instead of rolling. The road was laden with gravel and glacier dust that had settled into two ruts for car wheels, while the rest was piled into the center. The eight-inch mound of dirt scraped the crankcase and engulfed the little trailer wheel. It churned up great clouds of dust. Fortunately no one was following us except semitrailer trucks loaded with supplies for road crews and early settlers.

We would be traveling in British Columbia, Northwest Territory, and Yukon Territory before we touched U.S. property again. Even the Canadians knew very little about this vast area. From Dawson Creek, the 634 miles of raw wilderness held an enchantment and excitement that never diminished.

The first point of contact arranged for us was in High Prairie. We would make a big loop into a northeasterly direction designed to miss the rugged mountain area and the so-called prairie. It was literally a forest of scrub birch, alders, and some scrub spruce.

As we neared the loop, I noticed on the map a trail penciled in indicating a road had begun that would cut off this 75-mile loop. I could not be sure it was completed, so we veered right on what looked like a western ranch road but with no signs to indicate whether it was the Alcan Highway.

From a distance we noticed what looked like clouds that soon became a heavy haze, and suddenly acrid smoke filled the air. Small burning trees had fallen across the road. We turned off the intake air on the car vents and closed all the windows. My wife applied wet cloths across the mouths and noses of complaining children.

Dawson Creek was behind us and the Lesser Slave Lake area had no fuel, so there was no choice but to go forward into a smoldering, not yet burned-out forest fire with a wooden varnished station wagon. I stopped often to lift a burning, fallen tree out of the trail before we could go on.

After what seemed like an eternity of straining, watery eyes, coughing children, and silent parents, we emerged into a clearing. There were no fires ahead of us. Ahead we saw some small buildings and a little white church.

This was High Prairie — our one scheduled stop. Church services should be starting in minutes. We noticed some small log cabins and made arrangements with an elderly caretaker to rent two of them. We hauled in our luggage, dressed without bathing, and headed for the white church.

Inside, with only minutes to spare, we discovered we were the sole participants. Two young women, missionaries for the summer, told us all able-bodied persons were out fighting the fires.

"We were not expecting you to come when you learned of the fires," one missionary said. I told her our first knowledge of the fires was the inferno itself. "It's a miracle you are alive," she said matter-of-factly. "Stay here. We will be back and have services."

In less than 20 minutes they had garnered some elderly people and children. About 20 of us were singing out of the little red and white "Showers of Blessing" songbooks we had carried in the station wagon. We began to feel relaxed and grateful to God, who was indicating how important it was to stay close to Him for direction.

Back at the cabins, we were met by a grateful caretaker who talked continually while I prepared our meager but welcome dinner of canned soup, pork and beans, and Spam.

The children played, and when the camp chores were done we climbed into our bunks. The long northern days allowed only dusk instead of darkness in mid-May. In the faint light and with the smell of burning wood everywhere we slept until 8 A.M.

After breakfast we packed the car and started down the loop. We knew that somewhere ahead we had to cross the Peace River. The very name had a quieting effect on my spirit.

3

Coming Home

The Peace River did not live up to its name. Spring breakup had created a churning, muddy torrent that was overflowing its banks.

As we peered out the car windows at the frothing river, I looked for a bridge. There was none in sight. A small cabin had a large sign, "Ferry Crossings – $10.00 per car." In small letters it said, "At your own risk. Please take your place in line."

This day there was no one in line. I wondered where the so-called ferry was beached. Then I noticed a half-inch steel cable tied to a large tree and stretched across the river to another sturdy tree on the opposite shore. Two iron pulleys rested on the cable, and it was secured to a platform large enough to accommodate one car. It had wooden rails on two sides and rested on large jet airplane gas tanks.

The man operating the ferry appeared suddenly, put two planks on the platform opening, and told me to unload the family and drive onto the platform. "I had a fellow in a small pickup that dumped with his wife in it," he explained. "But it's safe – I don't lose many."

As the front wheels rolled onto the bargelike platform, the weight of the car made the platform's other end come out of the water. I had to pull within a foot of the end to accommo-date the one-wheel trailer behind us.

We swung into the current that was now acting as our ally, providing the needed horsepower. It was a ride to top anything at an amusement park — pitching and straining, while we clung to the rails and to each other. It seemed a long time before we reached firm ground on the opposite shore.

We soon learned that rivers and mountain areas with names like "Peaceful," "Swift," "High," "Low," "Destruction," "Phantom," "Carcross," "Deercross," and "Bear Creek," usually had no seeming relationship to the places we encountered. Also, it was obvious that the roads the engineers had surveyed were not the roads that were still in use. We were probably following trails of wolf, moose, bear, and caribou, who usually picked the easiest route with no concern for horseshoe curves.

As we wound our way into the Yukon Territory, I recalled the novels by Jack London, Zane Grey, and Robert Louis Stevenson that had brought the place into such fame. The Yukon River was still very navigable and a much-used source for moving supplies. After two weeks of traveling, the primitive comforts of the area made us reluctant to leave.

From the town of Whitehorse we drove into the moun-tains. Near the summit we encountered snow and decided to stop at a place that offered log cabins for rent. A huge Yukon stove, with pipes leading up out of an oil barrel on welded iron legs and with a crudely hinged door large enough to accom-modate good-sized firewood, provided heat for us.

My wife soon had mounted a clothesline to dry the chil-dren's clothes and underclothes — hand rubbed and scrubbed with melted snow. It didn't take long for any place we stopped to acquire the lived-in look.

As I lit my Coleman stove to fix supper, I accidentally ignited some spilled gasoline. Soon the whole stove was ablaze. With a container of gasoline attached to the stove, I envisioned disaster. In panic I yelled at my wife to open the door while I pitched the fireball out into three feet of snow. The snow quickly extinguished the flames, but when I offered to relight the stove, everyone was in favor of cold sandwiches and dried fruit.

The night had still more to offer when our Yukon stove with its hot pipes burned through the sagging clothesline my wife had loaded with drying clothes. We awakened to smoke and the smell of scorching clothes that had dropped onto the stove. We managed to retrieve everything before there was irreparable damage to our short supply.

We crossed the Alaskan border at Scotty Creek and proceeded to a town call Tok Junction. From here we could go left to Anchorage or take another road to Fairbanks. We headed for Fairbanks where we had agreed to meet with the pastors of our church and drive down Richardson Highway to Anchorage later.

The road to Fairbanks was not finished. The roadbed consisted of big crushed rocks. The 100 miles to Fairbanks took four hours and four flat tires. But we slept with sheets on our beds for the first time in weeks.

Our plans were to stay in Fairbanks overnight and leave, but we learned the spring breakup was now on (last of May) in full force. Roads behind us were swollen lakes. Streams and creeks were inundating bridges we had just crossed, and chunks of ice were destroying some small bridges completely.

We had nothing to do but wait until the waters were down again. We stayed in a tiny parsonage with the Thomas family, whose parents we had pastored in Oklahoma. There were four of them and six of us, and the house became a wall-to-wall sleeping and eating situation. "Anything to get out of the cold" was, and still is, a good Alaskan slogan.

We enjoyed our stay with the Thomas family. Their congregation graciously took us in and arranged to send to Anchorage several cases of canned vegetables and fruit via the Alaska Railroad—a love offering for us from the church.

After a week the Alaska Highway Patrol (with only one station for the entire area) assured us we could safely cross all bridges to drive to Anchorage. These reports proved to be erroneous. We later learned they came from people who were driving special vehicles like 4-wheel drive Jeeps, or army six-bys (six-wheeled trucks).

The stars and Northern Lights were giving way to longer days of late May as the midnight sun began to conquer the darkness of this majestic land. We decided to go.

We left early in the morning from Fairbanks. Periodically throughout the day we encountered delays because of one-way traffic in areas where ice and debris had been bulldozed just wide enough to allow one car to pass.

We began to look for lodging in the early afternoon and discovered there was none available in the Big Delta area, nor in Fort Greeley. Motel clerks told us there should be rooms at Rapids Road House, several miles ahead. We were already at an elevation above 5,000 feet, and it was cold. It was now about 4 P.M., and I was beginning to feel uneasy. Nevertheless, we drove on because there was no reason to drive back.

We anticipated a warm bed that night along the Black Rapids River, which tumbled in fury alongside the road. The elevation was near 8,000 feet. When we arrived at the Rapids Road House we found every cabin filled with men from a road crew. Fifteen pieces of heavy equipment were heading for Big Delta and work there. The clerk told me there was plenty of room at Paxson Lodge, another 35 miles ahead, and there would be no big road crews to fill the rooms. On we went.

As the shadows began to obscure portions of the road, it became obvious that the drivers of the 15 pieces of machinery did not need to follow the old road and so created their own. They had often broken through to treacherous hot thermals. Sometimes the surface was frozen for six inches with a crust that covered soft quicksand type gravel. All I could do was pick my way and keep the mainly traveled road in view as a compass for my direction.

I was beginning to feel a sickening feeling of defeat and was about to turn around when the car suddenly came to an abrupt halt, as if in the clutches of a huge unseen grip. And truly, I was in God's hand because He has ways of guiding us during times of testing. I got out of the car to find I was hopelessly mired in a soft area where heavy equipment had broken through and the crust that had frozen over was too thin to support our car.

My car and trailer were settled to the level of the bottom of the car doors. The night was very cold and getting colder — well below freezing.

I was so thankful for that bearskin coat the missionary from Africa had given me. It didn't make sense then. Now it covered my four small children.

I gave my wife my heavy coat, and my lined jacket was beginning to let the arctic air through. My teeth began to chatter uncontrollably as I looked for material to build a fire. There wasn't anything combustible in sight. I had books and magazines to help start a fire, but the spruce, willows, and alders I saw around us would take a lot of drying out before they could be burned.

We prayed that cold starry night, and I told my wife, "God would not let us go this far only to abandon us and let us die." While I meant this for her, I wanted to believe it myself.

We had hardly finished praying when I looked out across the tundra and saw a star twinkle and disappear. The star twinkled again, then disappeared. When it appeared a third time it stayed longer and seemed closer. The star must be the headlights of an automobile coming our way. It would disappear into low areas and flash light on the high places.

The Army six-wheeled truck that came to a stop a few feet behind us, looked like a heavenly chariot. The two young men asking, "What are you doing out here?" looked like angels.

26

They had been to Big Delta at a bar and were in shirtsleeves that belied the temperature.

When even that big truck could not budge us, they offered to take us to their road camp a few miles ahead. By now we were really feeling the cold.

One of the young men said, "There's a big Caterpillar tractor off to the side of this road if we can get it started."

The other young man snorted and said, "You can't run a Caterpillar," to which the first replied, "I ran a tractor on Dad's farm. Let me try."

I said to myself, "Lord, if You ever started a Caterpillar on diesel fuel in the frigid North, now is the time."

I heard him tinkering over in the brush, then I heard the engine turn over sluggishly. It coughed, coughed again, then began to go "puc-a-puc" in intermittent sounds, some of the sweetest music I shall ever hear.

After warming up the engine, he yelled, "I'm going to have to practice a while." I watched as he pulled levers and pushed clutch pedals while a 10-foot blade mangled brush and small trees in the circles where he was maneuvering the vehicle.

Yelling, "I'm ready," he roared to us, swung around, and backed to within a few feet of our car. The men flung a huge chain with a giant grab-hook over my front bumper, which looked too frail for the task. I could foresee the whole front end being pulled away.

At a given signal, the car, trailer, and all occupants literally leaped out of their miry grave. He pulled us to high ground but, with my car running, I noticed my gas gauge needle slowly dropping from a three-quarter tankful to empty, and the engine halted.

I suspected a gas line had been broken, but found instead a large gash in the fuel tank, torn open by a sharp rock as we were pulled free.

It was the middle of the night and, when they pulled us into the road camp with their truck, there was no place for us to sleep. The kitchen was warm and we huddled around a large oil cookstove. We were all suffering from exposure and nausea.

Around 4 A.M., the cook appeared to get ready for the road crew's breakfast. He fixed us bacon, eggs, toast, and hot coffee, which we tried to eat. A disturbed foreman knew he had a problem on his hands and told us we would be towed on to Paxson Lodge, some 30 miles ahead.

We will never forget that wild ride behind a huge road truck with a short chain and my foot riding the brake as we went up and down, across streams and muskeg. Sometimes I had to drive with one hand, and reach out with my left hand to clean mud off the windshield for a peephole. With no engine, we had no wipers.

But at Paxson Lodge, warm beds, roaring fires, and fried-chicken dinners made the nightmare of the previous evening disappear.

The next morning, I removed the gas tank, pulled its jagged edges together, and piled on acid and solder. That kind of soldering is not supposed to work, but it lasted for two years, until I sold the car in Anchorage.

On our way again, over good graveled roads, it was easy to see why it all happened. We could never have driven to Paxson Lodge on our own. If we had made it even to the road camp, we would have been unable to cover the remaining 30 miles to solid roadbed.

This had to be one of the most traumatic times of my life. It was also one of the most wonderful answers to prayer I have ever experienced. Through the crisis God had increased my faith in our mission and also my determination to let Him take over the difficult times.

It was a warm beautiful day as we came to the junction of Richardson and Glenn Highways, and a few more miles to Glennallen, where we stayed for the night.

The roads were new and smooth here. In some places in

the great horseshoe carved out of Sheep Mountain some 5,000 feet up, they were still blasting with not much concern for an occasional car that was halted for two or three hours while crews cleaned up the rock. A Caterpillar with a heavy blade often pushed debris aside and motioned us through with curiosity and impatience.

We had left the Sheep Mountain area and were on our way to the Matanuska Valley, which was still being framed on the Roosevelt cooperative plan. Suddenly I felt a literal "flushing" of my entire being with the presence of the Holy Spirit. Tears of joy began to flow. I turned to my wife, who was also crying. "Honey," I said, "we are coming home."

4

Growing Pains

Arriving in Anchorage on June 1, 1949, will forever be etched in my memory. First I managed to locate the "parsonage" by deduction — because there was no number on the building and it was the only house on the block begging for an owner to set a match to it.

The tar paper siding with matching roof had a wooden cross that sagged in a northerly direction. Evidently it had been used for some kind of radio antenna.

The paint was peeling from windows and doors, and the one-bedroom structure was sagging into the mud because there was no foundation. I drove quickly to the bank where I had been told there would be a key.

When I talked to the vice president of the National Bank of Alaska, he could not believe what he was hearing. Yes, they had a key and there used to be renters that deposited $100 a month. But for a family to live there? He shook his head.

The place had been purchased by a representative of the church several years ago for around $3,000 "furnished." No one from headquarters had ever seen it. We took the key and drove back to the parsonage only to find both front and back doors unlocked.

Our first parsonage and place of worship. The tent, donated by Dr. Powers and "Kankakee" college is on top of the car; the chain used to pull us many times is still on the front bumper. The tent became our temporary home until the building could be cleaned and repaired.

As we pushed open the door, field mice scampered across a floor covered with oil and soot from an antique stove that was overturned. A section of stovepipe was hanging from the roof jack in the ceiling. There was not a stick of furniture anywhere, and the layers of wallpaper seemed to wave at us.

The floor was rotten in places, and when I walked into the bathroom I actually fell through it. On one side of the bathroom sat an old tub that was not connected to anything. Water ran across the floor, which sagged toward a corner, and drained out.

The toilet was still connected but also was in danger of disappearing into the lower areas of the floor. Its chief support was the soilpipe. Lorene was following me, and all I heard was, "Oh, Honey," but that said it all.

I made arrangements to have Lorene and children stay elsewhere that night. I slept there alone, knowing I had a lot of work to do fast.

My first move in the morning was to go to the Alaska Railroad and arrange to have our furniture brought up and placed in the outside porch area, which had the best flooring. I could not afford to pay additional storage charges. It had been there a week already.

Now the squad tent would come in handy for sleeping and storage. It was daylight around the clock, and the canvas helped ward off the early June chill.

We threw everything out in a junk pile in the backyard. I placed plywood on the floors in the bad places and warned the children to stay out of the bathroom except when accompanied by a parent.

We pulled down wallpaper. I purchased a new stove and pipe from the hardware store that also supplied our oil for two 50-gallon drums outside the building.

I threw out the old tub and installed a metal shower. There was no need to turn on the hot water spigot, for there was still no hot water tank. Needless to say, one did not have to wait long for their turn to shower with water at glacial temperatures.

Part of our equipment included a sturdy hydraulic jack, and I began to try to level what was left of the floor joists with corners that had not rotted away. Working underneath, I had to dig and burrow to repair the joists with splices, a very poor and temporary repair, but time was important.

It was while I was underneath the house that I felt someone kicking my feet and saying, "Hey, are you Korody?" I slid out and a thin-faced, small man in baggy trousers with a big grin said, "I am R. G. Fitz."

I didn't recognize the name immediately, but soon I put some things together. This was Dr. R. G. Fitz, with 30 years experience in China as a missionary. He and Mrs. Fitz had fled the Communists and stopped by Anchorage to meet us on the way to Fairbanks. We put them up in our makeshift tent, and these beloved missionaries were our first Alaskan guests.

Dr. Fitz helped me labor, and Mrs. Fitz worked with my wife for two days before they headed for Fairbanks and then home. We had blessed times of fellowship and prayer and talked about our dreams for the interior of Alaska, where he would soon be going. He was rejoicing with us that God had allowed us to come and open up the coastal work.

Within a week, the place was beginning to look and feel more livable. Lorene even brought out her lace curtains.

I purchased supplies frugally and was disappointed to find the refrigerator we brought had a leak in the aluminum coils. All the Freon was gone, and people told me you didn't solder aluminum in Alaska because it required a special skill. God arranged for the only qualified technician in Anchorage, Homer Moseley, to repair our refrigerator. In the process Mr. Moseley told me he had a "very religious wife" who lived just down the block. Ruth Moseley became a member of our church for the rest of her life.

I ordered a metal sign painted saying, "CHURCH OF THE NAZARENE." With a string hanger on a nail it announced our intent and position in this frontier town.

We had 50 of the little red and white "Showers of Blessing" songbooks. With a dozen folding chairs and an old Kimball piano, we were in business for the Lord.

Our very first service consisted of four Korody children, who sang with books held properly, even if the two younger ones could not read the words. They substituted words from memory that sounded as if they ought to fit: "Sufficient for me since He died on the tree" became "Put some fish on for me!" We even took an offering that day and recorded it along with six in Sunday School and church.

By the next Sunday, I had placed "Showers of Blessing" on two local radio stations. Both were new stations and glad to get any kind of program that had good format.

The next Sunday a young construction worker named Lowell rapped on the door. We had the only church I remember where people knocked before entering. I wanted to leave the door open, but the spring weather was still too brisk.

The first congregation of Anchorage Church of the Nazarene: *(L. to r., back)* Matthew, M. R., Lorene; *(front)* Lewis, Jeannette, Ronald.

Later that Sunday came another knock, and I was surprised to greet a stout, middle-aged lady in a very broad-brimmed hat. Long strands of beads were draped around her neck to her waist. She was painted brightly, with a broad grin and a husky hello. I introduced myself and asked her name. "I am a Nazarene missionary," she replied. Me, too, I thought. I asked if she was acquainted with our headquarters in Kansas City. Her answer was, "I am a missionary of the Nazarene with headquarters in heaven."

With my construction worker and my missionary, we had eight the next Sunday and decided to put 10 percent of our first offering back for missions. The construction worker stayed for the summer. The middle-aged lady attended several Sundays and disappeared as suddenly as she came.

Slowly we grew and eventually our tiny front room was

crammed with 24 chairs and a piano that was moved into the kitchen when the chairs were set up. With continually more construction workers showing up and our canvassing the area gleaning four middler Sunday Schoolers, we were feeling so good about our growth that we rented the upper floor of the old Pioneer Hall at Sixth and F streets.

I had to clear whiskey and beer bottles, cigarette butts, and just about everything else from the Hall, which often housed dances on Saturday night. As I stood in the doorway, the Lutheran pastor's wife waved to me from across the street in their new church. "I don't envy you," she hollered. "I did that for over two years before we built here." Actually, she gave me fresh courage as I envisioned a lovely church building like theirs with our church name across the front.

We felt good about leaving our tiny front room and moving to Pioneer Hall. But when the summer of 1949 ended and snow appeared on the mountains surrounding Anchorage and temperatures began to drop, the summer construction ended and workers disappeared.

Just as the summer closed, the Milton Thomas family from Fairbanks came for a visit. With their two children and our four, we had 10 for Sunday worship instead of 30. It was obvious that when they left we would be back to my family, where we had started more than six months earlier. "What are you going to do?" Pastor Thomas asked. "I'll begin again," I said, "and at least I have a hall to worship in and a warm place to live for the winter."

I had put new siding on the house, repaired the floors, added linoleum, a new roof, and a small bedroom. Tar paper had also been placed against the outside of the house two feet up from the ground with dirt piled against it. There was not much ventilation because the windows could not be opened.

God began to regrow our congregation, even during that winter. A burly gold miner from Circle Hot Springs, converted under the ministry of Ben and Bernice Morgan, announced to us he was coming to Anchorage to help us establish the work. His name was Louis Johnson, and we helped him build a small cabin about five miles outside Anchorage. Building here was simple. A double wall stuffed with dried moss for insulation, four small windows, a roof jack for the stovepipe, and you were in for the winter.

Another couple, Heber and Iva Berry, came from Maine. They stayed with us until they were able to rent a log cabin. A month later they built a small home also.

Our first convert was a sharp-appearing young airman from Elmendorf Air Force Base. From the day Arden Sickenberger knelt at the chairs that formed an altar he was an inspiration to the now growing congregation. Eventually he became a faithful minister of God.

On one occasion four young construction workers of Greek descent who could not read English wandered into Pioneer Hall. Before they could adjust to the loud hymn singing of enthusiastic Nazarenes, Heber Berry grabbed one of them by the arm and seated them in rear chairs. I could see their consternation. They thought they'd come to a union meeting, and now the only exit was blocked by a burly, smiling Maine woodsman. They stayed for church and came back several Sundays. One of them was saved and testifies how a wonderful "mistake" brought him to Christ.

Soon another military man, Bill Williams, began attending. He was an army sergeant who had me driving all over Anchorage looking for a place to "buy" so he could bring his family to Alaska. I learned later he was just speculating on property that changed hands often and usually at a profit. Bill came to the altar one night, and after finding the Lord, laid down a deck of cards, a pair of dice, and a cigarette lighter. The truth came out in the confession — he was an inveterate gambler. Bill's life changed, and a happy wife and child joined him in Anchorage.

5

The Junkyard on E Street

I was driving Bill around when I first noticed the junkyard at 1220 E Street just across from the Chugach Elementary School. It was to be the future site of First Church of the Nazarene.

We needed to build, but I knew in order to purchase and establish credit, I would have to get something to let banks and businessmen know we were a bona fide denomination and I was for real.

I asked Dr. Powers for, and received, a general power of attorney. It was a very potent document, actually listing the entire assets of the Church of the Nazarene as cited in Dun & Bradstreet and making them available to me. (Dr. Powers instructed me to destroy the document when I was finished using it. I thought I had. When it turned up 25 years later, I gave it to headquarters. It is presently in the church archives.)

After I convinced Dr. Powers we had the right location, we bought the junkyard. It was just 11 blocks from downtown and at the exact geographical center of Anchorage.

My good friend, Bob Baker at Matanuska Valley Bank, helped us with our purchase. While Mr. Porta, the land owner, had offers from others at a better price, he was urged to sell it to us. When the bank loaned me $4,000 toward the purchase price, I knew God was working it out. Mr. Porta not only sold the property but also removed all the junk.

Getting the property approved for building was an unexpected hurdle. There was real opposition in the city council about having more churches in Anchorage's South Addition.

A small log cabin church located next to the home of a non-churchgoing councilman rang its large bell for five minutes every Sunday morning right under his bedroom window. Needless to say, he wanted no more churches near him. Our little group met in our home with much prayer and fasting concerning the situation.

Junkyard at 1220 E Street. Present site of First Church of the Nazarene. Chugach Mountains in the distance.

During this crisis I met one of my very best Alaskan friends, Earl Hillstrand. He was a young lawyer who became interested in my problem. Earl and I tramped the deep snows, wrote letters to people, and published a large article in the Anchorage *Times* — all this while my cigar-chewing councilman remained adamant with his statement: No more churches in the South Addition of Anchorage.

Anchorage South Addition was to remain a "Class A" restricted zone. God helped us get the necessary 51 percent of signatures of nearby property owners to build, but still no move by the council. I later learned that a lot of under-the-table maneuvers were in progress to stop us.

We, too, had some good moves. We were praying in our little cottage with some families, when the phone rang and my lawyer excitedly urged me to meet him at the public library. He had found an opinion accepted by the Ohio Supreme Court that fit our situation. When our attorney read the federal opinion to the council they bowed in defeat. The vote was unanimous to allow us to build. It was God's victory. They would not forget Nazarenes.

As I was about to leave the council meeting that evening, I raised my hand. "Yes, Mr. Korody," asked Mayor Loussac. "Mr. Mayor, we will build a nice church, and Anchorage will be glad Nazarenes have come to help build Alaska. And, sir, could I have a bell?" The mayor jumped to his full five-feet-two inches and shouted, "Rev. Korody, go build your church any way you want it!" A roar of relief filled the room with tension-breaking laughter.

With property secured and building permits issued, my next step was to contract an architect to work from sketches and prints I had obtained from Nazarene headquarters.

I wanted a flat-roofed church that could support huge snow loads. The snow would act as added insulation during long, cold winter months. Headquarters sent me plans that had been used to build a Colorado church. Four huge beams, 12 by 30, of laminated oak, would support the roof.

Meanwhile, I would have to be content with a basement church with an apartment on one end that could double for Sunday School classrooms if needed on Sunday. With all our inspections handled locally but approved in Seattle, building in those days was a challenge. Any commercial public building had to be scrutinized step by step. Since I had employed a local architect to revise our plans, it helped to tell inspectors we had an Alaskan working on the project.

Because our basement church would be approximately 36 feet by 80 feet, we had to bolt four 2 by 12 planks together with 3/4-inch bolts every foot. We used extra reinforcement rods between poured pilasters and footings massive enough to support a skyscraper. No wonder years later in the great 1964 earthquake not even a crack showed in the building made of concrete block foundation and stucco over siding.

The approval had taken so long that now I encountered another problem. It was September, and I could count on a month at most for outside building. I had placed our parsonage on the market, and it sold quickly. I was able to garner $7,500 cash for it, which was a good deal for the house we came to.

We moved into a one-room apartment with a bath and kitchen. Now there was no place to gather between Sunday services at Pioneer Hall. We decided to meet in another member's home for prayer services.

We faced still another hurdle when we discovered the city building codes had not approved concrete blocks, even with reinforcement between layers and poured concrete pilasters. I had found two young men ready to go back to the Lower 48 after working summer construction jobs. The men were really block layers but had to go to carpentry because of the code. They would lay my blocks if I could do it now.

That night I slid down into my basement hole. It seemed so large. Tired, feeling all the pressures, I was beginning to sense guilt over my predicament. Maybe I should have waited until spring — with the block layers waiting, the windows I had ordered due any day, a lumber company account coming due, and all the money in the bank allocated.

There was a mound of dirt in the area the pulpit would

later stand. I climbed up on it and began to pray and cry. I felt so alone — no church board, friendly superintendent, or warm neighbors. Even my wife and children seemed far from me in this need.

I began to thank God for keeping me this far, and He brought to my recollection a sequence of events, step-by-step from Oklahoma, up the highway, until now. "I don't know how, Lord," I said, "but I believe You will help me find a way." The Lord seemed to smother me with His presence. I stood and shouted to the universe that I would replace that dirt mound with a pulpit and declare God's promises are true.

The next morning, I hurried to Anchorage Sand and Gravel. A Dutchman named Krouse owned it at the time. He was anxious to sell the piles of concrete blocks the city had refused to let him use. While I was there he called the city building inspector but had no luck getting the blocks approved.

I was feeling discouraged after he hung up, when the phone rang. It was the city calling in an emergency. The only water supply, which came from a glacier creek, had been cut off. The wooden aqueduct pipe had rotted in a section beyond repair. I could hear the city official say, "Mr. Krouse, we know you have been forming concrete pipes for some time. Could we buy all you have?"

"But, sir," he said, "they are not properly cured and haven't been tested yet."

"Let them cure in the ground," the official said.

"What about my blocks?" he asked.

"We will OK all your blocks," was the answer.

I said, "Thank You, Lord. You move mountains and You crack wooden aqueducts."

I started our two young men laying blocks. They assured me they would finish in a week if someone would haul the blocks and carry them to the scaffolds. There was no one free to do it but me. I borrowed a flat-bed truck, loaded up blocks at Krouse's Anchorage Sand and Gravel, unloaded them at the church, and carried them to the scaffolds the workers had built.

We received a letter from evangelist J. C. Dobson (father of Dr. James Dobson), who was recovering from a heart attack in Bethany, Okla. We had shared some wonderful times in prayer with him and a good harvest of souls in our first Kansas pastorate.

Upon opening the letter and remarking how nice the Dobsons were to remember us, a money order fell out. I glanced at it and remarked, "Hey, neat, they sent us $12.00." I was more interested in the letter:

> Dear Korodys,
>
> With Jimmy so ill, I thought I would try my hand at selling new houses a Nazarene developer is marketing. I have never tried to sell anything in my life, but God directed us to this. Enclosed is our tithe from recent sales. This is the other tithe, for we promised the Lord if He would help us we would double tithe. We placed the first tithe in the church offering and, with so many needs we were aware of, we prayed diligently about the second tithe. God said, "Send it to the Korodys."

My wife was holding the money order. "Honey," she whispered, "it's not for $12.00, it's for $1,200!"

Later Myrtle Dobson told us that when Jimmy recovered and began to teach art at Bethany Nazarene College she was never able to sell another thing.

With this money, and funds from our own treasury, we were able to pay off block layers, ready-mix cement, and windows that had come from Seattle. I was also able to secure help from the Department of Home Missions that enabled us to hire roofers with hot tar who finished none too soon.

It was now October 1, 1950, and we had just shoveled the dirt back against the building after asphalting the outside of the blocks. That night the temperature dropped to below zero for the first time that year.

Whatever outside work had been done was all we were going to accomplish for this winter. Usually weather stays fairly comfortable until Christmas, but that October it never got above 15 degrees below zero.

Our cesspool and septic tank were installed, but we were still without a furnace. We had managed to keep the building above freezing inside with "Yukon" stoves and a fan blowing the heat across the rest of the building.

A Baptist deacon in the plumbing business was selling us a furnace that would be adequate for later building — 450,000 BTU, with thermostatic-controlled pumps and convector fins for the basement auditorium. All this came to $1,200 more, sold to us at cost.

I had ordered the furnace only after much prayer. My times in the prayer closet were more frequent with the added financial decisions. I would tell God as if He didn't know, "Lord, Charles the plumber says the furnace will be here any day now. He does not have the finances to handle it himself and has four children to provide for."

I had written Dr. Powers and mentioned the need for heat, trying not to sound too desperate but informing him we could not worship until a furnace was installed.

Not long after writing Dr. Powers, I received a letter from another good friend, R. T. Williams, Jr., pastoring in Oklahoma City First Church. The letter contained a bank draft for $1,200 — what we needed almost to the penny.

The letter explained:
An elderly saint in our church had put this money

aside for a memorial window in our church. While sitting beside Dr. Powers during an airplane trip together, he was telling me of your urgent need to have heat so you could worship in your basement church.

I felt impressed to talk to this widower who loved Christ and believed it would please God much more to have a memorial furnace in a pioneer Alaska church than a church window in this situation.

The same furnace is still pumping heat to Anchorage First Church 35 years later.

FIRST CH.
BASEMENT
1ST SERVICE
DEC 10, 1950

The basement church after three months. The trees were cut and planted in the snow for the picture.

Our piano was in storage. When we moved into the basement church, a brother and I manhandled it into a flat-bed truck. Getting it down eight stairs to a landing and then five more to the basement floor was going to take some planning, especially in January with temperature about 20 degrees below zero.

We decided to slide the piano down a plank. I would hold a rope and he would balance the lower end. The plan was working until I heard him grunt and say, "I can't hold it." That meant I couldn't either.

What a toboggan run. It hit the concrete-tile floor on its back and every key roared and danced individually until Liberace would have been inspired. A year later, when we could afford to have it looked at, the piano tuner remarked that the piano was in excellent condition and hardly needed tuning.

The old Kimball upright was still doing its job in a Sunday School classroom when I returned to Anchorage 25 years later.

On January 8, 1950, Anchorage First Church was organized with 22 charter members.

6

The Basement Church

Our basement church was truly a miracle, and we enjoyed every inch of it like a miracle ought to be. It was home and church for our family.

Many souls were warmed and blessed in the sanctuary, around the altar, and in our apartment bedrooms, kitchen, fellowship hall, and furnace room. God worked among His people, and space was absorbed gladly.

We got busy making some seating to go with what few chairs we had while the furnace was being bricked inside and out and pipes installed.

The benches were crude, and I had informed the congregation, that now had grown to more than 50 people, to sit on the bench they had constructed. It was one way I felt they would give more attention to safety factors. After all, second-grade lumber was guaranteed to snag hose, give off splinters, and create back problems. We had no time to sand them for that first service.

At last the boiler was fired up and the pumps were driving hot water through convectors. The black paint from the manufacturer was responding to the heat, and clouds of black smoke began to fill the basement auditorium. It was like clouds from heaven as we sensed the wonderful warmth that began to radiate through the room.

Our first service in the basement auditorium was December 10, 1950. I called the worship to order and began to lead them in singing from the *Showers of Blessing* hymnals. We felt like Ezra 3:10: "And when the builders laid the foundation of the temple of the Lord, they set the priests in their apparel with trumpets . . . to praise the Lord."

Our Maine woodsman, Heber Berry, his wife, and daughter sat on his hastily constructed bench. She became overcome with joy and started to shout God's praises, when a loud cracking sound joined the singing and shouting. Suddenly the family of three was sitting on the floor amid splintered lumber. Needless to say, that changed the order of the service.

A steady stream of servicemen began to respond to the invitations we gave at the two local bases. They could always be sure of having dinner with one of the half-dozen families now attending or could accept whatever they knew was baking in the rear of the basement sanctuary.

Seldom were there fewer than a half-dozen around our table, and sometimes as many as 25 overflowed to makeshift tables set up in the auditorium adjacent to the kitchen. We managed to have plenty for everyone, with the salmon we caught, potatoes from Matanuska farms, and the moose and caribou provided by the Alaska Railroad.

Alaska Railroad trains would often hit charging bull moose in the "right of way" plowed out for their routes to Fairbanks and Seward. The moose liked the easier walking in the plowed areas and refused to give up their "trail" even if it meant charging the train.

Crews followed the trains and stacked the undamaged portions of the animal, hide and all, at shoveled-out junctures. These had actually been prepared as an escape for the moose but were never used by them except for their cold storage.

We would hang these frozen quarters in our boiler room to thaw and then prepare them to cook. My wife fed a lot of young military couples who were on short rations, with these moose and day-old bread from the local bakery.

Our little congregation was self-supporting a year after we had organized — more than 10 percent of all our monies given to missions, a budget established for a zone college, and plans being laid for a parsonage for the pastor. Establishing First Church in Anchorage had cost the general church only $16,000, which included the salary for the Korodys, the trip to Alaska, the purchased property, and any monies to subsidize building.

In 1950 Rev. Lewis Hudgins, who with his wife and three children were in our Nome missionary work, asked me to come and preach to the Eskimos. What a beautiful experience being with these pioneers among the Arctic people.

While in Nome, I ate my first seal liver and tasted tom cod dipped in seal oil. My introduction to these delicacies came when I was invited to an Eskimo home for dinner. They had prepared their best — tom cod, muktuk (blubber) from blue whale, seal liver, whale flippers, and some salad (willow buds put down from last spring in salt brine).

After I prayed, they dug in with gusto. Chunks of tom cod were dipped in the seal oil and held in their teeth while a sharp knife whacked off the bite, expertly missing the lips, of course.

My host looked at me as I tried to figure out where to begin. His wife said, "Oh, Pastor, we eat raw and forget you don't." After rummaging in a back storage area, she emerged with a slightly rusted can of Van Camp's pork and beans. I breathed a sigh of thanksgiving. After using an old-fashioned knife-blade can opener, she set it in front of me with a broad smile of amusement over my solved problem.

Then she said, "Oh, I forget again. We use hands." There was no silverware in those early Eskimo homes. All eating was done with fingers. "Wait," she said, "I fix." An old box in the corner yielded a large army tablespoon, a casualty from an army mess kit.

"Not very clean," she said, so the accumulated tarnish and whatever was worked over with a corner of her dress (the inner lining of her long sealskin parka). "There," she said as she pushed it down into my waiting can of pork and beans. I had a good meal and blessed fellowship with these gracious people.

In Nome I learned new lessons in the joy of simple living. The Eskimo games included blanket tosses, dogsled races, and sliding down steep slopes on anything that would glide on the packed ice and snow. "Que Yanah" was a word I learned to use often, for I had much to say "thank you" for during those visits.

We had blessed services interpreted by Brother Hudgins. There was no need to interpret when prayer time came. The Eskimos expressed themselves freely with loud pleas indicating necessities coupled with bursts of joyful praise. No one was in a hurry.

A potbellied stove glowed red in the corner of the little church. With no ventilation and a packed house, I was picking up a lot of strange scents that seemed to affect no one but me.

I leaned toward Brother Hudgins and commented, "Perhaps they would like to take off those long, skin parkas and be more comfortable."

He laughed. "Don't suggest it," he said. "Some of these folk have little or nothing on under those."

My trips to Nome were via a reliable old C-47 plane left from World War II. There were no meals or beverages on board. In fact, the turbulence was so heavy that the seat belt felt good when we would lose 400 or 500 feet in some of the swirling currents.

Much of the trip was over the Arctic Bering Sea, and I noticed there were no life preservers in sight. An inflatable raft was lodged in front of the seats. There was no point in being concerned about rescue anyway if you fell into these waters. Survival was limited to minutes.

7

From a Mustard Seed

Anchorage continued to grow. Streets were paved and there were even some sidewalks between Fourth and Fifth Avenues. Our police force began to expand. There was an influx of people who did not want to work nearby gold-bearing streams at $32.00 an ounce when they could earn from $80.00 to $100 a day at expanding air force and army installations.

Young women with cameras on a strap walked Anchorage streets, alert for construction workers and servicemen. The cameras gave them the status of "professional photographers" and kept them out of the hands of the police, unless they were caught in the act of prostitution.

We were growing culturally as well. In October of 1950 the Anchorage Concert Association presented noted violinist Roman Totenburg, being assisted by equally famous Maxim Shapiro, in our high school auditorium.

Citywide campaigns included Jack Schuler and featured singer Stewart Hamblin, newly converted in the Billy Graham Hollywood Crusade, Hyman Appleman, Dr. Russell V. DeLong, and many others. All spoke several times in our church.

By 1951, other denominational churches were taking root across Anchorage. On Good Friday of that year, the First Presbyterian, Methodist, Nazarene, Lighthouse of the North, Spenard Chapel, Lutheran, Episcopal, Church of God, and Baptist churches held united services. There were lost souls enough for everyone to minister to, and the desire to absorb the influx of new people was a concern of every pastor. Missionaries love any group who lifts up Jesus.

Church growth in our own denomination was flourishing. The organization of the Alaska District and our first District Assembly will never be forgotten. Fairbanks, Anchorage, Nome, and Seward composed the district. We had begun in June 1949. Our first edition of the Alaska District Minutes (1951) records: "It is inevitable, of course, that our church should enter other cities of Alaska, of which Anchorage, the largest, had not been entered. A couple of unsuccessful attempts had been made earlier, but June of 1949 will be recorded as the birthdate of the church in that city. Rev. M. R. Korody and family reached Anchorage that month and the second Sunday started services in the tiny front room at the [yet still being worked on] parsonage."

Our assembly itself was unique. After two days of good services, with much prayer and fellowship, our first official board was organized. Dr. Hardy C. Powers presided in a side room of Fairbanks First Church with all people in a circle of chairs enjoying a very informal but dignified district assembly.

We elected elders and officers, and took care of business matters at hand. A look of deep satisfaction and affection seemed to radiate from Dr. Powers when he rapped a gavel on a chair and declared the first Alaska District Assembly adjourned.

The next meeting would be in Anchorage. I knew it would be a challenge to accommodate the guests because space in homes was a big question and hotel rates were much too expensive. But when the time came, it seemed no one minded the wall-to-wall sleeping in makeshift beds and sleeping bags. Moose, caribou, and salmon were abundant, and the fare was healthy and tasty.

An article, including an architect's drawing, appeared in the Anchorage *Times* (October 1951) with the caption, "The Parable of the Mustard Seed is illustrated in the accomplishment of the local Church of the Nazarene, who have now completed their first unit valued at $125,000 at the corner of 13th and E Street, designed by Taylor and Kilpatrick, local architects." The article also detailed plans for the coming construction of the beautiful upper sanctuary that would seat 250 people plus a choir of 50.

Our Sunday School in November 1951 recorded 100 persons. Tuesday women's prayer bands were well attended. As each mother in the circle of prayer finished praying (and she prayed until she was satisfied) she would arise from her knees and take over as relief baby-sitter in the next room. The attendant would then join the group in prayer until all had finished, more than two hours later.

It usually took a good supply of cookies and Kool-Aid to last out the two hours. Prayer with the children, Bible stories, and outside strolls, when weather permitted, made these Tuesday events a time even the children anticipated. It was like a continuing Vacation Bible School. We never lacked children. When older ones started school, there were babies continually filling the ranks.

Our NYPS programs were always exciting, with well-planned and well-rehearsed programs of interest to everyone. It was not uncommon in the preservice evening hour for the NYPS to give an altar call and the seekers and testimonies around the altar to become the evening service as well.

By 1952 we had reached 150 in Sunday School. On Easter Sunday, 1953, we had 194 in Sunday School and 200 in church.

At the District Assembly of 1953, Dr. Powers presided and Dr. John Riley of Northwest Nazarene College joined us.

Our host, Jess Morrison, served succulent king crab, which neither of our guests had ever seen. One of these huge spiny crabs with enormous claws when held by each hand and spread out, measured three feet.

I told them how delicious the crab was and, at that time, abundant off the coasts of Seward and Homer. Dr. Riley looked at this huge spider with its claws and sharp spines and, without thinking, innocently asked, "How do they propagate?" While his face suddenly turned crimson, and the women pretended not to hear, Dr. Powers, Jess Morrison, and I could not hold back our laughter as Jess, almost inaudibly, was heard to say, "The Lord knows." Dr. Riley decided against it and ate the rest of the lavish spread our hostess had arranged, which included king salmon.

In May of 1953, Louise Robinson Chapman came to Anchorage and endeared herself to us. She excitedly told us about her plans to pick up the fringe areas of missions by creating a fund to help missionaries meet any extraordinary needs. The fund would be separate from the regular General Budget that included all our missions. She would call it "An Alabaster Offering."

Our first use of Alabaster funds was the result of our call to headquarters when, after the walls on our Minnesota Avenue Church were up and the roof was on, a freak 100-mile wind scattered the building like matchsticks.

We had supported the new Alabaster program, and now we were to be recipients. Our own funds depleted, they lent us $500 to restore what was to be the second Church of the Nazarene in Anchorage.

We organized our men, pulled nails, sorted lumber that could be reused, and purchased new materials. In five days we rebuilt the entire structure.

A drunk who had passed by and had seen the debris of the partially finished church, came by a week later, sober, and confessed he had decided against alcohol.

He knew he had been "seeing things."

God never does anything in half measures. The corner lot north of our church on E Street was the site of a garage where cars were repaired. It caught fire and more than 50 percent of it was destroyed, so the owner could not rebuild or repair it. Being forced to sell, he found many ready buyers, some offering more than the $4,000 that was our bid.

I rejoiced when my friend, Bob Baker, the president of Matanuska Valley Bank, called and asked me to meet him in his office. It seemed the other interested buyer was heavily mortgaged to the bank, and in the liquor business. Mr. Baker was unwilling to lend him more money.

"Rev. Korody," the president said, "if you can raise $4,000 this afternoon, it's yours, but that's as long as I can hold it."

We had exhausted every dollar in our current building program. Trying to extract money from headquarters on that short notice was impossible.

Sensing my frustration, Mr. Baker said, "I'll give you the money for a month without interest." It had been his plan all along. That's how we got the corner lot.

We began getting our finances together for work on the superstructure. We elected to sell bonds using the top of weekly offerings for the "sinking fund" needed to redeem this municipal-type bond that offered 5 percent interest over a span of 15 years. We sold bonds to our congregation, but mostly to City of Anchorage people – including bankers and business owners. We also found estate money not being used, and people by now were taking note of our work and believed in us.

Our congregation was involved totally with Anchorage and her rapid development. We stated our views on radio and later on television.

I was now beginning what would be nearly a 10-year career (1953-63) on Channel 2 TV with a nightly telecast six times a week. The response from the beginning was very rewarding in contacts for the church and service to the community. It was called "A Closing Thought for Your Day" and lasted for seven minutes.

The program became so popular people began calling the station for spiritual help. We were not able to handle the load and eventually asked people to write their requests or phone the church office for interviews. I instructed the program director and engineer to cut off calls at a certain time so I could get out of the studio.

I was leaving one night when I was nearly run down by Charlie Gray, the engineer. "Pastor, I'm sorry, but I think you had better talk to this guy. He just will not quit calling in and won't take no for an answer."

The first words I heard were pitched in high excitement: "Pastor, my name is Charlie, and I listened to your telecast tonight. You said God had a plan for everyone and wanted to help you with it no matter how you feel about yourself. You said if anyone would appeal to Jesus for forgiveness and help, no one was turned down."

He continued, "I had just purchased two fifths of bourbon. I knew if I drank them, sooner or later I would be out like a light. If I did wake up, I would go into d.t.'s. Either way, I'm done for.

"I took the two bottles and went to my front cabin door and crushed them on a rock. Then I went back to my cot and knelt down and told God I was taking Him up on His deal. I said, 'Lord, let's You and me be partners in Your way of life like Pastor Korody talked about.'

"Something has happened to me," he continued. "This whole cabin is lit up like the sun was inside. My legs feel like a couple of feathers under me, but my head is clear and I feel so good I could climb a mountain. Now, Reverend, the reason I called you, I need your help. You don't have to come over here. I found this old dog-eared, beat-up Bible in a corner, and all I want from you is to tell me where I can find in this book what I've got."

I told Charlie where to look and prayed with him. The studio help listened and were awed by the event. They shared the story often in the years of telecasts ahead.

8

Never a Dull Moment

Our Rogers Park home was tiny but did have three bedrooms. We moved out of our basement apartment to give us room for our expanding Sunday School. We financed the project ourselves with an FHA loan and moved in even before the debris from builders was removed. We were the only house there at the time except for the family across the street.

Our living room would be so full of servicemen and guests for dinner on Sunday after church there was no room to come in except from the front door or through the garage. Once seated, guests didn't get up, and everyone was served from the end of the table. Occasionally someone had to climb over the sofa and behind the chairs to reach the bathroom. But we all enjoyed the moose, salmon, potatoes, gravy, and cabbage with day-old bread. Always 20 and as many as 30 stayed for dinner.

During our Alaskan ministry, we served as a delegate to General Assembly three times. In those days, even with my expenses paid, I had to borrow the money from my good banker friends to take my family with me to Kansas City. My wife's parents, who lived in Kansas City, would never have permitted me to come without their daughter and grandchildren.

It seemed the timing of the General Assembly (every four years) was about right — it took that long to pay off the old loan before I negotiated a new loan for the trip.

Part of the servicemen who attended church during the years. This picture was taken on "Servicemen's Sunday."

Returning from our first General Assembly in 1952, a pilot friend called me with some disturbing news. "I flew over your wilderness cabin and noticed windows were broken out and things strewn around the area," he said. "I think a bear got in."

I had purchased the cabin from a bush pilot who had suffered a tragic loss of his family and would not go back. It was on unsurveyed land and had cost only $600. I had three years to pay it off. The cabin was located on a beautiful lake I later named after my wife, Lorene. The salmon were plentiful in the lake and two streams.

The structure had a sheet metal exterior and an aluminum roof with a 10-gauge iron door. It had six 24 by 24 windows, and the bear had just walked in.

I said "walked" because when I arrived to inspect the damage, it was obvious what had happened. Snow had slipped off the pitched aluminum roof and piled up solid outside a window. He had pushed the glass in and with nothing to hold him from the scent of food, he squeezed through. His 700-800 pounds on the kitchen table brought it down. The collapsed table must have panicked him. It looked like the cabin's interior had exploded – stove and ice box overturned, dishes off the shelves and smashed, pillows ripped apart and chicken feathers everywhere. He exited on the other side through another cabin window, taking it out, glass and all.

Bears are very curious. With no human scent in the area upon his inspection, he made several returns, probably using the same means of entering and leaving.

He had found our stored "C" rations and with his own style of opening the cans had managed to eat a portion from each. He bit into a can of popcorn and had chewed it considerably but without enough reward to justify any more effort. He had also found the candy (marshmallows and peanuts on an upper beam), the peanut butter, and also margarine.

Bear odor was pungent, and I knew he was not far away. I went home and came back two days later. I was greeted by a fisherman using my canoe who said a pilot had dropped him and a girlfriend off to fish.

"Where is she?" I asked.

He pointed to the cabin and said, "She got airsick and is lying down in the cabin."

"Have you looked in on her?" I asked. "A big bear is in the area and the cabin is in shambles because of him."

He blanched white and when we found her lying on one of the torn-up bunk bed mattresses, it was no problem, sick as she was, to head for the door. I told him to stay alert and out of the bushes. They sat in the canoe in the middle of the lake until their plane returned.

My son Matt and I began the clean-up by throwing everything out the cabin door. We could repair and salvage later.

I had brought along two gallons of bleach, and when we were down to the linoleum, we doused the floor with massive doses of water and bleach and swept it out. We repeated this until the place looked and smelled better.

All day we worked, repairing the table, sewing pillows, and putting usable dishes back on shelves. Finally, even Matt admitted he was tired. There was still quite a junk pile outside the door that still had to be buried. I knew from what I had seen and the descriptions of pilots who had seen the bear that he was huge and probably young. I don't think an older bear would have risked reentry to the cabin.

It would never be safe again to bring my family of four small children back here to play around the cabin. The bear would not attack them purposely; but if he were surprised, he could be counted on to do unpredictably what bears do.

I heated some soup and, although very late in the evening, the sun was high. We ate little but lost no time in going to bed.

I awoke with the sun lower but trying to rise again. It was late June and daylight around the clock. Seeing my son asleep, I grabbed a fishing pole and decided to catch a few trout for breakfast.

I was about to return with my rainbow trout when I heard the iron door bang against the cabin. I assumed Matt was up and decided to join me fishing. I called out to him, and he answered me from a point in another direction from the cabin.

If he was over there, who was slamming the cabin door?

There was only one answer, and I yelled to Matt to stay where he was. I was going to the cabin to try and get my rifle.

Seeing nothing resembling bear as I crested the embankment with the cabin in view, I ran a record 100-yard dash,

Cleaning silver salmon—a part of our "survival" food.

opening the door, and slamming it shut with myself on the other side.

Grabbing the rifle hanging on a nail, I moved a cartridge into the barrel, ready to fire. Then it came to me — I was safe, but Matt was outside and defenseless. There was nothing to do but cautiously peek out and pray for God's protection on my son.

I yelled, "Are you OK?"

There was a sense of relief in hearing him reply, "He was chasing you, but he is upstream at the bend of the creek."

Matt said I had gone within 50 feet of him. I was so close he did not see me as he stood up to his seven-foot height and sniffed the air for a scent of me.

We had a small boat. I climbed in and knelt in front while Matt paddled me toward the last place he'd seen the animal.

Suddenly he appeared about 150 feet in front of us, crossing the narrow creek. I aimed and fired quickly from the moving boat. My shot was not fatal. With a roar he started across the creek. I knew I had to stop him and placed my 220-grain bullet into his front shoulders as he was broadside. He went down, got up, and went into an alder thicket. He tore up the area as if the alders were matchsticks. He was now breathing heavily, and I could hear him moving toward us in the tall grass opposite the cabin.

Matt was trying to turn our boat around. I had no paddle to help. He had the front of our boat caught in the current and resting against the bank. We were not more than 50 feet from where I could see the tall grass moving and hear the bear's groans and heavy breathing.

I was trying not to panic as I jumped to the shore and pushed us around, heading toward the cabin.

Safely back at the cabin, we watched and listened for 30 minutes, and all was quiet. I asked Matt to climb a tall birch tree and look around.

"All I see is a dark puddle of water in the weeds over there. There's no bear, Dad."

I knew he had to be there somewhere, but we decided to have breakfast. After a devotional time with our Bibles and prayers of thanksgiving for God's protection, we went fishing again, so we could take some fish back with us.

We got into the boat and went up the lake on a stream that emptied from the Mount McKinley area. We paddled downstream into a creek that was full of beaver and three different varieties of trout.

As we turned into the creek, Matt stiffened and whispered

hoarsely, "Dad, I told you he wasn't dead. There he is!"

I looked downstream and saw another large bear. He was looking us over, too. Momentarily I wondered if he might be right, until the bear decided to scamper and leave the fishing to us for now. I knew he was healthy and sound of limb.

Later, when we were in the plane, I showed Matt his puddle of water. Our huge black bear was lying broadside in the tall grass. A busy summer, fall, and winter would pass before I looked at him again the following spring.

When I finally did go see the bear a visiting district superintendent from Arizona was with me. I told him the story and took him over to the cabin. He collected the huge claws that were bleached out, and I took the skull. Animals, wind, rain, and sun had cleaned them all to an ivory white.

Our services were running around 200 in 1954. We knew we were in for some adjustments that year, for Dr. G. B. Williamson would be replacing Dr. Powers as our general superintendent.

Dr. Powers felt we were not ready for district supervision because we operated out of an Advisory Board, and he visited us twice a year (which was as much as any district superintendent could have at that time). He knew the heavy expense of a district superintendent would drain the funds needed for new work.

But our next general (without any hint of what was coming) appointed a man from Florida as our district superintendent. Our new D.S. flew to Fairbanks and came to Anchorage via train on what I thought was a mild day. He emerged in a wolfskin parka and introduced himself. He was a good man with thin Florida blood who was very bewildered with the raw vastness of the area. We were to become good friends, and his tenure of leadership on the district was a great source of fellowship to us.

The district superintendent had lots of things to attend to in that area from Juneau to Anchorage, Seward to Fairbanks, and Nome to Whitehorse in the Yukon Territory. Whitehorse was added because it was closer to Alaska than anything organized in Canada.

The job involved a lot of bush flying into all these areas, where the laying out of plans and projects was vitally needed. The problem was that our district superintendent was also in supervision of a district in Canada and lived there with his family. He was actually no closer to us than Dr. Powers in Kansas City.

When our problems needed the attention of district leadership, it was not easily available. Finally the church, after many of our pleas, helped bring the district superintendent to Alaska to live.

As Anchorage grew, we began to have a steady flow of visitors from civilian areas. A baker, a Maine woodsman, a gold miner, and a carpenter and their families were our first civilians. Now they were coming from all occupations—schoolteachers, policemen, employees of the *Times* and *News*, a member of the legislature, and others from the city of Anchorage. I was always so grateful to hear the shouts of victory and to see the tears of joy when our altars would fill up with seekers.

Our ministries diversified to meet the needs of our new people. We always had a large group of men praying early Sunday morning and a servicemen's prayer group Saturday night. (They slept in the church, and we had coffee and rolls on hand.) Our Thursday-night calling groups ministered to people who had been in Sunday services, and our women's prayer group met every Tuesday. Every service was full of joy, and our music was lively and well prepared. We felt, and it was evident, that if people came once they would want to come back.

By April 1955 we had 263 in Sunday School and 300 in worship services.

9

The Last Frontier

On May 8, 1955, we dedicated our new building. More than 300 people attended, including church and city officials. The Anchorage *Times* featured a picture of the crowd and services on the front page.

As we look back, no one seemed as excited about the number of people coming as they were about what was happening in our midst.

"Showers of Blessing" on radio and "Closing Thought" on television six nights a week were giving us exposure in the Greater Anchorage area, and now into smaller cities and villages via satellite.

Our responsibility in all this made us aware of our needs to represent Christ properly. We were laying building blocks, and Jesus, we knew, was our bedrock Foundation.

On January 9, 1955, we celebrated our fifth anniversary. Approximately 161 people had united with us by profession of faith. With students from our church now in four colleges (many of them ex-servicemen), we were enjoying the flavor of a church on the growing edge.

Things were beginning to change in the whole picture of Alaska. The big issue was statehood.

Dr. De Long's visit
1951

A visit from Dr. Russell V. DeLong *(r., front)*, well known in the Anchorage area as the speaker for "Showers of Blessing" radio.

Territory leaders were pro and con on the question, which was now the subject over every coffee cup. It seemed the interior of Alaska, the Panhandle, and most villages were opposed to statehood. They were beginning to see too many changes already with constant traffic coming up the Alcan Highway and daily flights to the lower 48 states.

Anchorage, which was the access hub, was very pro-statehood and made every effort to convince the rest of Alaska. Slogans, banners, and speeches laced with the advantages of statehood were common.

America's last frontier was vanishing. Aggressive building replaced the spirit of adventure and call of the wild. Log cabins disappeared and business establishments or apartment buildings replaced them. Our first two "skyscrapers" featured neat apartments and office space rising above 15 stories.

While the progress was inevitable, we viewed it with a tinge of nostalgia. The old-timers lamented that Alaska would never be the same again. Though the majestic scenery remained unspoiled, the change of traffic proved they were right.

Our 1956 district assembly was held in the Seward church with our new general superintendent and district superintendent presiding. We now had eight churches in our district. Our scrapbook, with a copy of "The Alaska Nazarene," records the average attendance in worship: Anchorage — 300; Fairbanks First — 247; Fairbanks Totem Park — 47; Juneau — 47; Ketchikan — 150; Nome — 118; Seward — 106; Sitka — 50. One can easily see the growth of Alaska indicated in each of these figures.

The June 6, 1956, issue of the *Herald of Holiness* contained an article called "The Alaska Frontier" as told by General Superintendent G. B. Williamson. It capsulated his view of what was happening in Alaska. I believe the North was rubbing off on him!

Roy F. Smee, now in charge of Overseas Home Missions, had never been to Alaska. He was getting close to retirement, and I knew he wanted to come. I suggested to our board that we invite him to visit us. He accepted, and we had good services.

Dr. Smee expressed a desire to do three things in addition to leading a revival in Anchorage First Church. He wanted to: (1) see the Matanuska Valley, site of the early settlers; (2) see the Kenai Peninsula and our work there; and (3) go on a short fishing jaunt.

Some of the men in the church decided to go along on Dr. Smee's home mission tour to Kenai. We used a new 1956 Plymouth and headed southward on the newly gravelled road toward the Kenai River area.

The gravel flew and rocks bounced off the inside of the

fenders with force even undercoating could not subdue. The speedometer was registering 70 mph on long, straight stretches. We were making good time around curves blasted out of solid rock a few feet from the lapping ocean waves.

Eventually Dr. Smee asked, "What's the hurry?"

"We're racing the tide," the driver explained.

Suddenly the car swerved to a dead stop at a clearing by the ocean's edge. To the dismay of our guest, the fellows began peeling off white shirts and ties and pulling on coveralls and boots. From the trunk of the car they grabbed buckets and climbed down a 30-foot ladder to the beach below. It was razor clam season, and we had decided to include the prized seafood on Dr. Smee's tour.

An hour later, we climbed the ladder with full buckets and made our way sheepishly back to the car. Dr. Smee was whittling on a stick with a small pocket knife. Without looking up, the shavings flew. "Home mission tour?" he muttered, grinning and raising an eyebrow. All was forgiven, and we continued to Kenai.

Dr. Smee had also expressed a desire to see the Matanuska Valley. A new paved highway had just been completed, and I thought it a good idea. I could not accompany him but gave him a car to use and ample instructions on how to get there and back from his hotel.

About an hour before the evening service, I stopped by to see how our evangelist was getting along. I found him still in traveling clothes, sitting on the bed with his head down.

"You will never believe this," he said. "I still haven't seen the Matanuska Valley."

It seemed Dr. Smee had made a wrong turn and found himself at Elmendorf Air Force Base. Because my car had a special pass glued to the windshield, he was waved on. He soon found himself away from the military buildings of Elmendorf and spotted what looked like a four-lane highway. "That has to be the road to the Valley," he reasoned and started down the right-hand side. Suddenly the air was full of the shrill sound of sirens. Two military police cars were bearing down on him at top speed. He was ordered out of the car, told to lie on the ground, spread-eagled, and not to move.

The hoarse voice of an amazed sergeant was asking, "What are you doing on the jet fighter strip, my good man?"

After what seemed hours, he was finally able to convince them he was harmless, even if he had done something so unbelievable as to drive a car down an airstrip. To complicate matters, it was a "secret fighter strip" where camouflaged fighters and pilots were ready for instant alert signals from the Strategic Air Command.

"Fortunately," Dr. Smee explained, "the M.P. was from Oklahoma. I heard him tell the provost marshall over the phone, 'I believe him. It's so dumb it has to be the truth.' "

The police escorted him off the base just to make sure the pilgrim from the Lower 48 didn't have any more problems.

I had also promised my evangelist friend we would fish at my wilderness cabin, just a half-hour by float plane out of Anchorage.

The morning we decided to go was beautiful but heavily laden with ground fog. We warmed up a borrowed Cessna 180 plane on floats and, with my wife along, were finally cleared for takeoff. Since we had no report on weather conditions in the cabin area, we were surprised to discover a "socked in" condition (fog) around the cabin that would not let us land. We flew around looking for a "hole" somewhere on Lake Lorene to no avail.

Our guest was beginning to feel uneasy, and I decided to try another lake where there was usually a breeze. We found a good-sized "hole" in the clouds, and I landed the plane. We taxied to a stop by a neat little cabin.

"Hey, this is nice!" Dr. Smee said.

"Oh, this isn't our cabin. He is just sitting here until we can find ours," my wife answered.

Later in our own little cabin over some nice rainbow trout and black coffee, my friend confessed that trout fishing by float plane was not what he thought it would be.

10

"Without Me Ye Can Do Nothing"

Our next home was not everything we had hoped for, but it was spacious. It had a large full basement and a beautiful picture window in the bedroom that opened to the Chugach Mountains. We put a Ping-Pong table downstairs for our growing children. It doubled as a large serving table for food at Sunday dinners. We served 50 guests after church one Sunday — that was in addition to what our other members were doing in their homes. As usual moose, salmon, Matanuska Valley potatoes, and cabbage helped make it possible.

Our upstairs had a living room with oak floors and a lovely kitchen. It was much different from the tent pitched on Fourth Avenue, and we thanked God. We had room for a piano, which never seemed to be silent.

While we were in this home God gave us the opportunity to minister to a Catholic family who had not attended church for years. They were within easy walking distance of our building, so I encouraged the parents to let the children attend. One son, Robert, won awards in Sunday School and seemed especially to enjoy it. He had an eye disorder that caused him some problems at school, and he was definitely a loner.

One day while the father was away on business in Seattle, Robert and his mother became embroiled in a heated argument over a matter of discipline. When Robert's mother threatened to spank him and tell his dad, something inside Robert broke. He ran downstairs and came back with a loaded .22 caliber rifle. His mother ran from the house and Robert shot her as she fled to the car parked outside. He then shot his little sister who was sobbing at the front door, and then his younger brother who was fleeing to the neighbors.

After his arrest I was the only one Robert would see. He could not tell me why or how it happened. He begged me to intercede so he could attend their funeral. He was only 13 years old.

Robert was sent away for psychiatric treatment and detention in Washington, D.C. I kept in close touch with him for four years. During this time of rehabilitation, a large tumor was discovered on his brain. His erratic behavior was the result of the pressure it exerted. The tumor was removed successfully and, four years later when he was 17, he was declared competent to make his way in society.

Now the question was: Where do you put a minor who would not be considered an adult for another year, and not of legal age for four more years? There had to be a reliable sponsor who would keep him until his 18th birthday. No one volunteered. After prayerfully sharing this with my wife and children, we elected to open our home.

It took a little while for both our family and Robert to adjust. Much credit goes to Lorene and the children, who opened their hearts and shared their lives with a convicted murderer.

Many of my friends and parishioners were not happy about this decision. They did not want him in worship and Sunday School with us. The scars of that horrible nightmare would never be erased, but Robert believed Jesus had forgiven him even if he and some other people could not. Eventually Robert went to a good vocational school and then worked in his dad's shop.

In February of 1958 I was asked to pray for 34 people who were becoming citizens of the United States in a beautiful ceremony at the Federal Building. The occasion was another first for Anchorage and for a lot of people present. It was thrilling to think we were receiving citizens into the United States, and Alaska had not achieved statehood yet. I believe it was indicative of the spirit of Alaskans and their faith in our country.

The ceremony brought back a lot of memories for me. I am the son of an immigrant. I was only four years old when my father was studying his required lessons — portions from Lincoln's Gettysburg Address, the Preamble of our Constitution, requirements for voting, and the Oath of Allegiance to our flag and country.

I remember my sisters, who were 10 years older than I, becoming exasperated with Dad when he stumbled over words in broken English. I don't think we considered that he already spoke in several languages, and the English language was the most difficult.

Dad had come over in the hold of a ship in 1906 to Ellis Island. He went West at the turn of this century and helped build the Union Pacific Railroad. In 1910 he homesteaded on railroad land in Lemmon, S.Dak. He sent for Mother and built a sod hut on this beautiful prairie land that still had small herds of buffalo. There were Sioux Indian encampments all around.

All this came back to me as I looked upon the people waiting in the judge's chambers to become U.S. citizens. Many of them had fled Communism and had come to this Territory of Alaska to make their home.

When my parents homesteaded out West, they were not interested in just surviving. They were enduring hardships as a way of life, knowing this land was theirs and they were free to develop it. The Alaskans were never afraid of hardships either; they were creating wonderful ways of life and home for the thousands still coming.

And come they did! By now, sister holiness denominations were scrambling for property in the areas surrounding Anchorage. I showed property and offered suggestions about lots and blocks still available. But the prices were beginning to reflect the market and many buyers, in their desire to economize, would buy back lots in poor access areas. This would retard the growth of the church, and in some cases permanently relegate it to oblivion.

The lines were drawn, and it was clear where the traffic would flow. Choice lots on now busy corners and streets were still available but were being picked up quickly by businesses and investors who were watching the zoning laws.

The newcomers needed to consider that if property was easily accessible and business was after it, that it was exactly the kind of property needed for church growth. Some of the best advertising can be a cross on a church right in the path of the man going to work, the housewife on her way shopping, and the weekender off to the lake.

Our 1957 notebook speaks of stability and progress. In April there were 221 in Sunday School and more in church; in May, 237 in Sunday School. Now our church board was showing 80 percent civilians and 20 percent military. We were not reaching fewer military but were picking up the civilian population at a ratio of four-to-one as they began the trek to Alaska.

It was in 1958 that our busy schedule was slowed to a grinding halt.

The nightmare began one evening when I was emptying a hunting rifle in my bedroom. The house was filled with a deafening explosion, and I heard my wife scream. Running to her side, I saw three-year-old Ileana standing over her sister, who had been doing her homework in a corner overstuffed chair.

My gun had been pointed toward the outside of the house, but when I inadvertently activated the trigger I had moved just enough to catch the corner of the living room where my teenage daughter was sitting. The bullet had gone through a bedstead, a wall, an overstuffed mohair chair, and shattered her arm between the elbow and shoulder, lodging, in fragments, just an inch from her heart.

To this day I don't understand why it happened. Maybe it was to slow me down from a schedule that was taking me away from my wife and family. Even though we'd always been a loving, laughing, and praying unit, I'd become too busy. Six TV programs a week, building funds, calling, counseling, civic involvement, including clubs and two ministerial associations—I was not spending the time I needed with them.

Now our beautiful, talented daughter, who had never brought us anything but joy all her teen years, lay dying in a hospital. My grief was compounded by guilt over this accident at my hands.

I can still see her with a bolt through her elbow held up by a pulley, looking at us with her lovely smile. "I'll be all right, Mom and Dad," she'd say. The presence of God overwhelmed us with His comfort and assurance.

Somehow priorities stay in place in such an hour. Our people rallied and took over the household and church. One member, our Sunday School superintendent, even went to our home and patched the holes in the bedroom and living room walls.

Our doctors were the best and, while skeptical in the beginning, began to be believers as they watched Jeannette's progress. After the metal had been removed and the bone fragments in her arm began to reknit, her worst problem became infection.

That thick horsehair arm on the chair had slowed the bullet and saved Jeannette's life. It also brought the contamination of the dead horse with it. The doctors were stumped in knowing how to treat it. Slowly, very slowly, the infection left.

God was using Jeannette in her testimony to the doctors, her friends, and her church, who loved her deeply. Many people of this group began to call on God again or look to Christ for the first time.

Her doctor, who wrote the case up in a medical journal, visited with me 10 years later while in Anchorage. After serving as a surgeon in the Korean war and doing research in orthopedic surgery, he still refers to this as one of the phenomena of his medical career. He admits it was "Someone besides himself," and then jokingly adds, "She did have the best of doctors."

We watched the X-rays with awe as bits of bone less than the size of a pencil moved into place and connected. Nerve ends began to reassemble. The day finally came when the pin in her elbow was removed and her arm put in a new cast.

Jeannette had been our church pianist and was taking lessons from the Baptist church choir director. She was not home a full day when she bent over and touched the keyboard with the tips of her fingers sticking out of her cast. "I'm going to play again," she said calmly.

I knew she would. Jeannette sang and played her way through Pasadena College, where she was elected homecoming queen. She is still a vibrant Christian who has accepted all that happened much more easily than her father.

God used this near tragedy to give me a better grip on my ministry. I found a new feeling of gratitude for my children, for Lorene, and for friends who were there when we needed them. The scars would heal, but they will always remind me of the words of Jesus, our Lord and Savior, "Without me, ye can do nothing." I say, "Amen."

God allowed still another big lesson in my life in 1959. It happened one night after I'd delivered a late telecast and returned home. Lorene always waited up for me, and we usually retired around midnight.

This particular evening I felt uneasy. Around 2 A.M., after two hours of tossing, I dropped off into a fitful sleep. I awoke suddenly with excruciating chest pains, my neck and lower jaw hurting, and beads of perspiration forming across my forehead.

No one needed to tell me I was having a heart attack. I could hear my wife breathing in deep sleep next to me. I panicked, thinking, "I have to get out of bed. Lorene must not wake up in the morning and find herself sleeping with a dead husband."

I tried to get up but couldn't move. The attack was having a stroke effect, too. With all the effort I could muster, I managed to roll over on my side away from my wife. I did it again, and the next moment found me on the floor with a thud that awakened her.

It was very early in the morning, but my dear friends, Drs. James and Virginia O'Malley, summoned two heart specialists to my hospital bedside. Four days later, my reports said, "Angina brought on by physical exhaustion." I was confined to complete bedrest until I would be told differently. I knew I wasn't indispensable, but it was a critical time for our church with the building program plus six telecasts a week.

I prayed earnestly for healing and strength. I promised God (and Lorene) that I would find rest stops. I had realized that the world would not break a step nor lose much sleep if I suddenly disappeared from the scene.

Two weeks later, I was back into my schedule, but now with an afternoon rest that seemed to be a wonderful remedy.

Besides a time of learning, 1959 was a year of victory. This was the year we anticipated statehood. I use the word *anticipated* advisedly because there were pioneer people who were very slow to respond to the drumbeat of Anchorage for this change of status.

We began stacking wood and anything flammable (except auto tires) into a growing pile in the park areas between Ninth and Tenth Streets.

The mounting woodpile that was being prepared for the day we achieved statehood was a real temptation to some of our Anchorage teenagers. The fire department was called to the spot several times to put out a blaze before it got out of control.

Statehood ceremonies, 1959. M. R. Korody *(seated, second from left)*, who prayed for this new state and its future.

We had a half-dozen policemen in our congregation by this time. The burly red-haired sergeant mentioned to me in the course of conversation, that among the crowd enjoying the firemen putting out the blaze were some of our church teens. Two of them were my youngest sons, and two more were my Sunday School superintendent's children. They were fine boys but mischievous, and I knew this was presenting a temptation.

Finally, statehood did come and both newspapers headlined, "WE'RE IN," on June 30, 1959. The huge bonfire could be seen across Anchorage.

11

This Is Your Life

In January of 1960 the church surprised us with a "This Is Your Life" program. How they managed to do it without us knowing is still a mystery. But we were genuinely surprised.

When we came to the evening NYPS hour and walked into the new multipurpose room, a huge map of Alaska and the United States covered the platform area. Streamers from Anchorage were pinned to cities across the United States. From each city was a letter that had been bound in a keepsake book. As we sat on the platform a parishioner read them all aloud.

We wish we could print all the letters in this book. However, here are some that represent a cross-section of sentiments. These are still some of our most cherished possessions.

In September 1949, in an Air Force uniform, God was merciful and forgave me of my backslidings in old Pioneer Hall, Sixth and F Street. I joined the church when they organized in 1950 and answered a call to preach under the ministry of Rev. J. C. Dobson, evangelist, in 1951. I never handled as many concrete blocks in my life as I did with Brother Korody. Since leaving Alaska, I have finished my training, am an ordained elder, and continue to serve God and my church.

Thousands of miles and over seven years of time separate us, but we are still bound by the ties of the Holy Spirit that brought us together. We were saved in Fairbanks out of the gold camps (Circle Hot Springs) of the Interior under Rev. Ben and Bernice Morgan.

How can I forget your invitation to live with you in that tiny, two-bedroom home on 430 Seventh Avenue. With our four and your four, there was wall-to-wall living of 10 people until I got my cabin built on Raspberry Road. Moose, bear, salmon, caribou helped until I landed a job at Alaska Railroad shoveling (by hand) whole carloads of fuel to feed hungry boilers and hungry kids.

How can I forget God's call to the ministry under the preaching of J. C. Dobson in 1951, and eventually pulling up roots and heading for our college at Pasadena, Calif., or those services at Pioneer Hall and our basement church we all sacrificed to build – a "temple in the wilderness." Perseverance, integrity, and love of our Christ made it "all joy," even when we were sweeping up cigarette butts, beer bottles, and litter of every imaginable nature from the dance the night before at Old Pioneer Hall. I am now pastoring in Nevada.

December 1950, a lonely Air Force boy landed in Anchorage [Elmendorf Air Force Base]. I don't even remember who invited me, but I attended a service in old Pioneer Hall in March 1950, and in that first service I knelt at our chair altar, and God for Jesus' sake forgave me of my sins. You folks treated me like parents, and I spent more time in your home and in services than I did at the base. I was sanctified and called to preach in 1951. After my tour of duty and completing college at Bethany, what a joy it was to come back to Anchorage with my wife and pastor our second church.

How can I forget our congregation's sacrifice to build the Kingdom. Many months I held back money for soap and razor blades, and all the rest went into the building program.

> Still pastoring with ammunition stored from those battles.

I was born in California of parents who owned several saloons and gambling houses. My mother was saved when I was five years old and would take me to street meetings in front of my father's saloons.

When my marriage broke up after pastoring for several years, I went to Anchorage as a carpenter. How can I ever forget our first meeting when I rapped on your door in 1950 and your hospitality included me in your evening meal, which was the first of many. How I remember when the summer crowd went "outside" and that November Sunday when there was just your family and a half-dozen left of the 40 on the previous Sunday. Someone among the 10 of us left (including our family of 6) asked, "What do we do now?" You said, "We just keep knocking on doors and letting everyone know we are here and why we are here."

I remember Zechariah's prophecy, "But it shall come to pass. *At evening time shall be light.*"

> Am back into a fulfilling ministry
> A former lonely carpenter

[He went out and started many new Korean churches in California.]

I came to Anchorage in 1950, a Maine woodsman and fisherman. Unsettled but married to a saintly ordained elder, we responded to a tug of our hearts to go to Anchorage and help out with the new work we heard was opening.

We arrived after an arduous trip over the highway with a half-eaten bear roast, which was placed on Mrs. Korody's table with your salmon and Matanuska Valley potatoes and lettuce. What a joy it was to share many meals in that tiny house until we found a cabin in Mountain View.

Our prayer meetings in the Mountain View cabin, the struggles of Pioneer Hall to basement church to upper structure with all the hurdles of new zoning laws, building codes, fighting time to secure a place to live and worship from elements we knew had to be reckoned with.

It has gone quickly. How blessed and glorious were those 10 years.

We were an Air Force couple with two little girls and caught up in the social whirl of military life that included lots of drinking. When we moved to Spenard, we would not admit that we were alcoholics. Our front yard was so littered with beer cans you could not see the walkway to the front door. Neighbors invited our little daughters to Sunday School. When they were dropped off after church, they would be singing choruses the pastor taught them in front of the church altar every Sunday morning. My neighbor [the Maine lumberjack's wife], when she learned of my birthday, embarrassed me by bringing a cake, but it started me thinking.

One night the pastor called on us and began to share with us the riches of a Christ-centered home and family. How can I forget the living room scene as my husband and I gave our hearts to Jesus. We confirmed this at the church altars (bench with a Navajo blanket thrown over it; truly a mourner's bench). Later we surrendered our lives completely in that tiny living room. We learned how to be parents.

[Their children are now in leadership in our church.]

Not yet 18 years old and headed for the bars of Anchorage. God had other plans and a soldier on the way to church asked if I would like to go along. The services and a meal in your home afterward were the beginning of a changed life.

I am retired from the service and do custodial work in a small Oklahoma town. I remember our services, the hunting trips you took me on to secure winter meat, and tending nets on the beach for salmon needed for winter meals. I went to Germany from there and around the world, but my life would never be the same. The church gave me the place I needed as a layman. We have enjoyed sharing this with our children.

I have often said, after years of serving my Lord, there are only two places I get homesick for — Alaska and heaven.

When I found myself in Anchorage for several years, they have to be the most memorable of my life. I had planned to spend the summer in Palmer with my brother but found myself most of the time in Anchorage helping in the exciting ministry of Nazarenes who would develop love and friendships that would endure a lifetime.

An Oklahoma Housewife

I came to Anchorage as a crewman on a merchant marine tanker in 1952. My purpose was devious, to say the least. I was going to use the church as a shield and attend while I sold and distributed narcotics. I was raised in a Nazarene home, so I knew the mechanics of the church program.

I had put God out of my life, I thought, but little did I know His plans for me.

It was Wednesday night, and I knew they had an evening service. As I descended the stairs leading to the basement church, I learned the prayer meeting was over and "Work Night" had begun. I was greeted by someone who introduced me to the pastor's wife, who, in turn, handed me a bucket of paint with a brush and smilingly pointed to an unpainted corner of the building. Afterward we had sandwiches (moose) and coffee.

From there I never caught my breath. My plans went up in smoke when I found myself at the Sunday morning altar of the church asking God to forgive me and guide me. I had some real problems getting back on track. My old associates were ready to kill me. I actually didn't fear them. I knew I had life in Christ that would never end.

I continue to serve Him with a beautiful wife and three children these years later in Oregon. As a local preacher and still true to my vows I can say, "His promises are true!"

My teen daughter's polio (Bulbar) was so deadly, so infectious, but you were willing to go into her room and pray, play your tape recorder of NYPS services and voices of teens wishing her speedy recovery.

She did recover and today is the mother of her own beautiful teens. As a young couple in the Army, you and the church helped us in our attitude and relationship to the church and God. We shall always be grateful.

Sidney, Nebr.

1954 and an Army recruit and his bride came to Alaska and Fort Richardson. I was Lutheran, my wife Nazarene. Neither one of us knew the Lord in a born-again experience. We decided to look up the Nazarene church. We were under conviction for salvation in that service but did not go forward. You were in a citywide crusade with Dr. Torrey Johnson and no evening service. That night we went forward under the big tent between Ninth and Tenth Streets, and you knelt and prayed with us as God mercifully saved us. The next Sunday evening we were wonderfully sanctified in your services.

You had a healing service and my wife, suspected of having cancer, was wonderfully healed. The dreaded symptoms are gone.

We have been teachers, Sunday School superintendent, missionary president, and board members ever since. Your training was good.

Oklahoma Couple

I was in your church until 1956. As a very young man, I came to Alaska while you were in the basement church. I was so moved in that first service, I came to the altar, gave my last $50.00 to the building fund, was called into the ministry, and haven't had any money since! You became second parents to me, and the church became my life and still is.

A Pastor in Washington

I came to the old Pioneer Hall and, after several services, one morning I laid my tobacco, a pair of dice, a deck of cards, and a cigarette lighter on the altar chairs lined up in front of the hall. You helped me find housing, and I brought up my family. As a cook in the Air Force, I still enjoyed many meals at Mrs. Korody's table.

A Couple from North Carolina

They shared the darkest moments of my life, giving me encouragement and strength to become a woman. For four years they were father and mother to me. I was a Christian teen then. Now I am a successful career woman but am not a happy woman. I know if I had stayed true, I would be a fulfilled person today. They are still "my pastor and his wife."

A Court Reporter in Newport News, Va.

[Thirty years later we shared again in a crisis with this lovely lady. Now married to a very prominent attorney and mother of two children, she looks to our Lord and is picking up the spiritual background she left behind.]

I was a young airman leaving Elmendorf to hitchhike to the Nazarene church. On the way, Ted and Gordon picked me up. They, too, were on their way to the Nazarene church for services, dinner, and fellowship. This kind of schedule never stopped for the next four years. I found myself at the altar giving my heart to Christ. He called me into the ministry. I was sanctified here. Went to work in soul-winning outreach and every other opportunity you opened. I met and married a girl raised in First Church. Our first baby was born and dedicated there. Off to Trevecca College and ministry. We love you dearly.

From Nashville, Tenn.

"How many are the lost that I have lifted? How many are the chained I've helped to free? I wonder, have I done my best for Jesus? When He has done so much for me?"

Afraid to live, afraid to die. God used you and First Church to give my life new meaning. I wondered, after those happy years in Anchorage, if we could stay true and continue to be victorious.

You told us if we looked to God and not to man, the words of Jesus would help us through everything.

We miss you all so much and yes, His promises are true.

A Couple from Alabama

We found you in your church office and poured out our hearts to you. Our military pay was fouled up, and we were broke. You got us a tiny apartment and furnished it with necessities; next, some boxes of groceries with fish and wild meat. Then you asked, "How are you kids fixed for money until your first paycheck comes in?"

In Anchorage, we became rooted and grounded in the Lord.

Sister Korody, with her sweet, quiet ways, won my heart. She is what one looks for in a pastor's wife — kind, gentle, and always ready to help. It was your example that stirred me as you spoke on missions and made me realize these were "Other Sheep." Just being near you helped. Now I am trying to help others.

From Jacksonville, Fla.

Easter Sunday evening, 1958, we went forward before the preaching started and were both wonderfully saved. Our horror visions of icebergs, igloos, and frozen North had all melted around Anchorage First Church people. How we would like to be with you tonight. We remember getting sanctified there under the anointed preaching of Dr. D. I. Vanderpool you had for revival. It has not been easy, but it has been Easter ever since. We will meet you in the morning over there.

From Lake Charles, La.

I was a teen girl in Germany engaged to a boy attending your church. You agreed to sponsor me and, after much red tape and complications for you, I received my permanent visa to enter the United States. I did not marry that young man (he had been in Hitler's S.S. troops and was working at that time on Eklutna tunnel near Anchorage).

I married a fine Christian in this area, and we both thank God and you folks for sponsoring me.

I was a Chinese boy from Los Angeles, lost in a maze of uniforms and adjustments from a Chinese area of L.A. to the frozen North of Alaska. I remember the G.I.'s lined up waiting for the "OK, dinner's ready," and found myself scrambling with the best of them at Mrs. Korody's table.

I remember distributing *Heralds* and the multitude of tasks we found ourselves involved in. It was here God called me into full-time service. It was here I learned more of cross-culture living and even brought a Japanese Buddhist to church who found the Lord.

Assistant Pastor, First Chinese Church of the
Nazarene, Los Angeles, Calif.

In June 1959 I came to Anchorage, a student at Pasadena College, for summer work.

I was having mixed emotions about a beautiful girl I left behind at Pasadena, and dating girls in First Church was beginning to trouble me.

I finally went to you for counseling and explained that my hang-up was because she was Spanish and my folks were a little concerned about our dating.

How I remember you asking, "Do you know if you love her?" I said, "I do."

You said, "Go home, get on your knees in front of her and ask her first to forgive you for taking so long to do it, then propose immediate marriage." It was wonderful advice, and I took it.

Pasadena, Calif.

We remember from office correspondence, then a visit in person, the many problems we faced there — the hundreds at the altar, the remarkable work, your position at the evangelistic center of Anchorage, the beginning from scratch. May God continue to bless you.

Roy F. Smee

In 1949 I appointed Rev. and Mrs. Korody to open the work in Anchorage. History has proved this was divine direction. The church is fortunate in having these godly people, true shepherds, as your leaders there.

Dr. and Mrs. Hardy C. Powers

Wish it were possible for me to be there. I join a loyal, appreciative congregation in saying this would have been impossible without loyal and consecrated leadership.

Rev. and Mrs. Korody have proven themselves faithful, loyal, unselfish, and above all, God's people for this task.

Rev. Bert Daniels
District Superintendent

I remember my visit in 1959. Congratulations to two wonderful people and their lovely family. They have a warm place in my heart.

We depend on the Korodys and expect them to continue to glorify God.

Louise R. Chapman
General NWMS President

The Korody family in 1958: *(Standing)* M. R. and Lorene; *(Seated)* Lewis, Matthew, Jeannette, Ronald, and Ileana, born in the Territory of Alaska, 1956.

12

Time for a Change

On August 28, 1960, Alaska Methodist University opened its doors and three of our church teens were among the first 100 enrolled. We had helped raise a lot of money to build a liberal arts college and hoped to see it equipped with Christian teachers. The first president was a Methodist pastor and an Asbury graduate, which made us feel comfortable in enrolling these students, one of whom was my oldest son.

Before the first year was completed, however, it was obvious we needed to make a change. I didn't mind seeing the Russian newspaper *Pravda* dropped off regularly in large bundles for students to consume in their Russian language courses. It did concern me when I learned one professor spent time defending and extolling the good points of Marxism without even comparing it to the Christian position.

We had high hopes the school would be a haven for conservative students who came from churches where alcohol, tobacco, and Hollywood were not guiding forces.

The university didn't turn out that way, though, so the next year we decided to help our students to enroll in a Nazarene college.

The December issue of *Alaska Nazarene* reported:

Anchorage First: 215 average attendance in Sunday School in November; 250 in morning worship; and 200 in evening service; 12 by profession of faith; $1,000 in Thanksgiving Offering.

Minnesota Avenue: 77.18 percent gain over last year.

Average attendance for district, 837.

All the churches on the district, now numbering 11, spoke in the reports of building, building, building!

Building a place to worship, building a flock to strengthen each other, building a wall of prayer and love around our people, fighting against time and elements that allowed no hesitation once the plan was in motion. Rain, snow, cold, darkness were predictable. Rain, sunshine, and victories broke into the calendar. I have told people it was not from spring breakup to end of summer we did our best work, but rather in the deep snows and cold of winter.

The daylight hours of summer had to be industrious in getting ground dug, concrete poured, roof on, fuel for heating in, fish caught, meat put up, and ore mined. The coming and going of people made for lots of adjustments in teaching staff, choir personnel, and other plans that never skipped a beat as far as long-range plans were concerned. When winter snows crept down the Chugach Range in October-November, everything was back in place.

Christmas 1962 found our oldest son, Matt, in his fourth year at Pasadena college and married; his sister, Jeannette, was a sophomore at the same school.

We were too strapped financially to bring them home for Christmas, and it really hurt to know they would not be with us. Fortunately, Matt's grandparents in Kansas City sent for him to spend the holidays there, and Jeannette spent Christmas in the home of good friends near Redlands.

Our two sons in high school were getting ready for college. Funds and distances from our school were a great concern. Years earlier, when I asked Dr. Powers what would happen when our children were ready for college, we were

91

assured the church would make a way. However, with our two older children, it was an extreme hardship. It would be years before their school loans would be paid.

At the time of our appointment, we were sent by the Board of General Superintendents and Foreign Missions as missionaries to open the coastal work in Anchorage. Later, we were shifted to the Department of Overseas Home Missions.

This shift changed our status and made us ineligible for funds that Foreign Missions earmarked to help missionary children.

After much prayer, I knew what God was directing us to do. After the first of the new year in 1963, we resigned but promised to stay until a new pastor was called. The morning we resigned was one of our most emotional times, even if it didn't show. The congregation implored us to take a long paid vacation. But that wasn't the answer, and God has the grace to provide the way.

By now our records showed nearly 500 members, most of them by profession of faith. Approximately 3,000 people knelt at the altars during these 14½ years. Thirty-five ministers came from this congregation. During the time after our resignation, we were besieged by friends outside the church asking us to stay. Businessmen offered lucrative postitions in the Anchorage area and other parts of the state.

I was grateful to them all. But God had called me to be a pastor; I would be a pastor until He called me home.

Now in addition to the daily priorities, we were all praying about the search for a new pastor. The district superintendent was patient and the board was in no hurry, but name after name had been called and no one selected by April.

After exhaustive effort, the board one day in meeting heard a member say, "I heard the pastor from Seward is going to resign. He is a good pastor and has a lovely family. Maybe he would be our man."

He was a wonderful man with the spirit of Barnabas, and

all felt he could be the answer if he would consider staying in Alaska. A unanimous call delighted him and his response was, "I accept the will of the people as the call of God."

Now that the choice was resolved the transition would be smooth. He would have two months to pack and put his house in Seward together, and we could easily get our things ready for overseas shipment. It all went remarkably well. The day after we moved out of our parsonage, he moved in.

None of us in our family could speak much about leaving. Close ties in our congregation were beginning to make us "weepy" already. Our departure day was set for June 16, 1963.

We heard from all our good friends. There were many phone calls and invitations to dinner. Letters and notes came from television viewers I had never met. Even some state and city leaders wrote to express their thanks and best wishes.

Suddenly all these relationships were coming sharply into focus. We'd been so busy growing Anchorage we didn't realize the strength of the ties we had there. Now we would be leaving it all.

I knew I would have to start over again wherever we went, and it would never be like this anywhere else. Yet we felt a peaceful confidence that we had made the right decision. My friends in Alaska would always be friends.

It was a beautiful spring, with green grass showing through the snow. With spring breakup, we made some final trips and even picnicked in the melting snow down toward the Kenai at Cooper Creek. We tried to memorize the beauty and stared enough to last our lifetime.

We were approaching our final Sunday. Morning services would be held in First Church, but evening services would be held in Central Junior High Auditorium. The mayor, members of the Ministerial Alliance, leaders in the community, and other church denominations would be sharing with us. Our members and all the teens and children had parts planned. I knew it would be a very difficult time. I can face hungry lions more easily than I can say good-bye. My family was feeling it, too.

It was Saturday morning, and I went out to collect the two daily papers. I would be meeting with the men for our 6 A.M. prayer meeting just as we had been doing for years. Heretofore, I never opened the paper; but before I threw it inside the door, I noticed the name "Korody" partially rolled into a fold and bound by a rubber band.

As I unfolded the paper, I couldn't believe my eyes! Headlines declared Sunday, June 13, 1963, as "Rev. Korody Day." Both papers carried the banner headlines and a proclamation.

At first I thought someone was playing a trick on me with bogus newsprint. There alongside of the article, in both papers, was this proclamation:

- "WHEREAS, for the past 14 years, Anchorage has benefited from the religious leadership of the Rev. M. R. Korody, pastor of the First Church of the Nazarene, and
- "WHEREAS, during his first years in Anchorage, Rev. Korody served as a leader in many civic and community affairs, both in state and local levels, and
- "WHEREAS, because of his outstanding place in the community, he was chosen to lead the nation in prayer for Alaska during the official statehood ceremonies, and
- "WHEREAS, Rev. Korody has been honored to serve several terms as president of the Anchorage Ministerial Fellowship, and
- "WHEREAS, in spite of his many activities, he has found time to be a good father to his children, Matthew, Jeannette, Lewis, Ronald, and Ileana, and
- "WHEREAS, it has been with the help, love, and understanding of his devoted wife, Lorene, that he has become one of the community's best-loved citizens, and

94

- "WHEREAS, Rev. and Mrs. Korody have consistently demonstrated the best in the American way of life,
- "NOW, THEREFORE, I, George Sharrock, mayor of the City of Anchorage, do hereby proclaim June 13, 1963, as

REV. KORODY DAY

in the City of Anchorage and urge all citizens to join me in paying honor and respect to this clergyman."

What is there to say? I felt undeserving but very grateful. Our reward was complete. Our cup was running over.

Those last services were deeply emotional. I received a framed copy of the proclamation, sealskin-bound letters from the teens and church, gold nugget tie tack from my juniors, and many other gifts that are still worn and on display. They speak to me of a period in the church when we were privileged to serve under God's wonderful timing.

Finally the last services were taped and filmed, the last telecast was over. Our eyes were wet with tears that kept coming as we departed from Anchorage that week and headed toward the Matanuska Valley.

The road going into the mountains was now paved and smooth. Soon we would be boarding the Malaspina Ferry for the inside passage trip south.

I had not accepted a church as yet. We were all weary and wrung out, too emotional even to pray like we wanted. But as we came to Sheep Mountain, the same God who had spoken to us about our apprehension in June 1949, spoke again, in June of 1963, "Lo, I am with you always."

We didn't have a place to go, as we did in 1949 when I turned to my wife and said, "We're coming home." But we brushed the tears aside and smiled at one another. We'd learned a lesson about home in the last 14 years. In our Lord and Savior Jesus Christ, we were already there.

First Church of the Nazarene, Anchorage, Alaska, 1959. Complete, except for the west wing. From man's trash (the junkyard of 1949) to God's treasure.